INTRODUCTION TO PL/SQL

FARHAN ALI ARAIN

To ask for any sort of help, or to give your comments, please mail me at the farhan.ocp@gmail.com

For my beloved parents, their love encouraged me in all aspects of my life and for my respectable teacher Madam Moomal Ali Pandhiani, who taught the subject PL/SQL initially and guided me in selecting my carrier.

Contents

1 INTRODUCTION

In this chapter you will learn about

What is PL/SQL?
 PL/SQL Block Structure
First executable program

What is PL/SQL?

PL/SQL is a procedural language; PL/SQL combines the data manipulation capabilities of SQL with procedural language capabilities (declaring variables, using conditional control structures and using iterative loop structures).There is no need to declare different data types in SQL and PL/SQL.
One can declare PL/SQL variables by referring to a specific column of a table which improves productivity and maintains.
PL/SQL improves performance of SQL by bundling SQL statements and by sending the whole SQL bundle to SQL engine in data base while the PL/SQL statements within PL/SQL block are processed by PL/SQL engine that is local to the client.
Without PL/SQL oracle processes one SQL statement at a time but by using PL/SQL the whole PL/SQL block (may containing many SQL statements) is send to oracle server for processing which drastically improves performance.
In PL/SQL program units like procedures, functions and packages can be declared
Which can be saved in compiled form on database server so further calls are efficient
And network traffic is reduced.
Pl/SQL supports object oriented programming by Object types which we will cover in coming chapter in detail.

PL/SQL Architecture

Pl/SQL statements are compiled and executed by PL/SQL engine, the PL/SQL engine can be at the client application as oracle forms or it is in the oracle server.
When a PL/SQL block is sent to PL/SQL engine it processes the PL/SQL statements and sends the SQL statements to the oracle server for further processing as shown in the following figure.

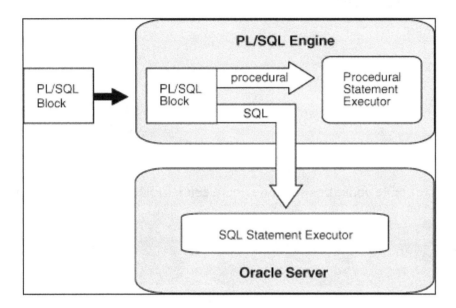

PL/SQL Block Structure

PL/SQL is a block structured programming. A block is the most basic unit of PL/SQL.
Block can be anonyms or named.
Anonym blocks are used to write the code where it is needed and executed, while named
Blocks are saved with specific name and are called at the place where their functionality is required and can be reused, Covered in detail in a coming chapter.
One block can be nested in other block (Nested blocks).
A block structure is shown below for an anonyms block.
An anonym's block has following three sections.

Declaration
Executable
Exception handling

Declaration section

This section is used to declare identifier like variables, constants, cursors, types and so on, this section is between DECLARE and BEGIN keywords.

For example

```
DECLARE
V_emp_id NUMBER;
V_emp_name VARCHAR2(30);
V_dept_constant number:=20;
```

Executable section

This section contains the executable code; this section is between BEGIN and END keywords.

Example 1

```
BEGIN
    SELECT  emp_id,
            emp_name
    INTO    v_emp_id,
            v_emp_name
    FROM    emp
    WHERE   deptno = v_dept_constant;
END;
```

Exception section (Optional)

This section is used to trap the exceptions in a controlled manner.
A specific action can also be taken with a specific exception covered in detail in a coming chapter; this section is between EXCEPTION and END keywords.

Example 1

```
EXCEPTION
    WHEN NO_DATA_FOUND
    THEN
        raise_application_error (-20100,
                                'No row selected for the specified department'
                                );
END;
```

The first executable program

Before executing any PL/SQL block in ISQL PLUS you should know about DBMS_OUTPUT.PUT_LINE.
DBMS_OUTPUT is an oracle supplied package and PUT_LINE is a procedure in this package.
This procedure is used to print an output. Before using this procedure, you must have to execute SET SERVEROUTPUT ON at SQL prompt as following.

Example 1

```
SET SERVEROUTPUT ON

BEGIN
    DBMS_OUTPUT.put_line ('This is my first programe');
END;
/

Output
This is my first program
PL/SQL procedure successfully completed.
```

Example 2

```
DECLARE
    v_emp_id            NUMBER;
    v_emp_name          VARCHAR2 (30);
    v_emp_constant      NUMBER          := 7900;
BEGIN
    SELECT empno,
           ename
    INTO    v_emp_id,
            v_emp_name
    FROM    emp
    WHERE   empno = v_emp_constant;

    DBMS_OUTPUT.put_line (v_emp_id);
    DBMS_OUTPUT.put_line (v_emp_name);
END;
/

Output
7900
JAMES
```

Summary

In this chapter you have learned that PL/SQL is a procedural language and PL/SQL is a block structure programming.
PL/SQL combines the procedural language capabilities with data manipulation capabilities of SQL.

2 GENERAL PROGRAMMING LANGUAGE FUNDAMENTALS

In this chapter you will learn about

Character Set
Lexical units
Delimiter
Identifier
Literal
Comments

Character Set

PL/SQL program is written by using a set of characters, the character set that PL/SQL uses are as following

1. The upper case A..Z or lower case a..z
2. Symbols ( ) + - * / < > = ! ~ ^ ; : . ' @ % , " # $ & _ | { } ? [ ]
3. tabs, spaces and carriage returns

Lexical units

Groups of characters make line of PL/SQL , these groups of characters are called lexical units, lexical units can be classified as following

1. Delimiters
2. Identifiers
3. Literals
4. Comments

1. Delimiters

A simple or compound symbol that has special meaning to PL/SQL is called a delimiter, For example + sign is used for arthritic sum.
Simple symbols consist of one character; a list of simple characters is given below

Symbol   Meaning

Symbol	Meaning
+	addition operator
%	attribute indicator
'	character string delimiter
.	component selector
/	division operator
(	expression or list delimiter
)	expression or list delimiter
:	host variable indicator
,	item separator
*	multiplication operator
"	quoted identifier delimiter
=	relational operator
<	relational operator
>	relational operator
@	remote access indicator
;	statement terminator
-	subtraction/negation operator

Compound Symbols

Symbol	Meaning
:=	assignment operator
=>	association operator
||	concatenation operator
**	exponentiation operator
<<	label delimiter (begin)
>>	label delimiter (end)
/*	multi-line comment delimiter (begin)
*/	multi-line comment delimiter (end)
..	range operator
<>	relational operator
!=	relational operator
~=	relational operator
^=	relational operator
<=	relational operator
>=	relational operator
- -	single-line comment indicator

2. Identifiers

Identifiers are used to name PL/SQL types and program units like procedures, functions, packages, variables, types and cursors.
An identifier should always start with a character and can be followed by numbers, characters, dollar sign or underscore. An identifier cannot have hyphens, slashes, spaces as following

```
--var&temp   Not allowed because & sign
--var\temp   Not allowed because \ sign
--var temp   Not allowed because space sign
```

Note: that and identifier can be of maximum 30 characters.

Reserved words

Some identifiers are predefined in PL/SQL and have some special meaning, these cannot be redefined.
For example you cannot declare the following variable because BEGIN identifier is already used by PL/SQL that indicates the start of the block

Begin NUMBER;

3. Literals

A literal is an explicitly provided value that is not and identifier; a literal can be number character, string or Boolean value. For example 1 is a number literal; 'A' is a character literal.
In the following example 'A' is a literal

Example1

```
SELECT 'A' literal
FROM    DUAL
/
Output
Literal
A
```

In the following example a string literal is shown

Example2

```
SELECT 'She said "My heart is as cold as stone"' lit
FROM    DUAL
/
Output
LIT
------------------------------------------------------
She said "My heart is as cold as stone"
```

Note: that the literal can be used in many place not only in SELECT statement, for example these can be used in where clause, in having clause, in assignment of PL/SQL etc.

4. Comments

Comments are used to give remarks in any place in code, to describe the functionality of that particular code.
Single line comments are given by using - - hyphen two times
Multiple line comments are given be enclosing the comments like following
                         /* comments*/
The following example shows the use of single line comments.

Example 1

```
--This select statement shows the use of the literals
SELECT 'He said "Life is like licking honey from a thorn."'
FROM    DUAL;--dual is used for the syntax completeness
```

The following example shows the use of multiple line comments

Example 2

```
/*This select statement
shows the use of
the literals*/
SELECT 'He said "Life is like licking honey from a thorn."'
FROM    DUAL;--dual is used fot the syntax completeness
```

Summary

In this chapter you have learned that PL/SQL language is written by using many characters called character set, Groups of characters make line of PL/SQL , these groups of characters are called lexical units, lexical units can be classified as following
1 Delimiters
2 Identifiers
3 Literals
4 Comments

Exercise

1. indentify decimeter and literal in the following statement

```
SELECT empno,
       'A'
FROM   emp
WHERE  sal > 8000
/
```

2. Identify identifier in the following PL/SQL block

```
DECLARE
   v_empno   NUMBER (10);
BEGIN
   SELECT empno
   INTO   v_empno
   FROM   emp
   WHERE  sal > 8000;
END;
/
```

3. Is this identifier "v_variable_employees_emp_number" correct?

3   PL/SQL DATA TYPES

In this chapter you will learn about

What is a data type?
Predefined PL/SQL data type
Variable declaration
Variable initialization
Scope of a variable in PL/SQL block

PL/SQL data types

A data type defines the format, constraints and valid range of values.
Every constant, variable and parameter must have a data type.
PL/SQL provides many data types and subtypes.
A subtype is a subset of another data type (called base type), a subtype have same operations as its base type, but only a subset of its valid values. Subtypes provide compatibility with ANSI/ISO types.

Predefined PL/SQL Data Types

1. Scalar
   These contain Single values with no internal components.

2. Composite
   Data items that have internal components and those can be accessed individually.

3. Reference
   Pointers to other data types, Explained in coming lesson of Ref cursor.

4. LOBs
   Pointers to large objects that are stored separately from other data items such as   text, graphics, and images.

Note: In this chapter we will learn about scalar data types only.

Predefined PL/SQL scalar data types and sub types

Category	Description
1. Numeric	Data type that is used to define number variables, constants and parameters.
2. Character	Data type that is used to define character variables, constants and parameters.
3. Boolean	Data type that is used to define boolean variables, constants and parameters.
4. Datetime	Data type that is used to define datetime variables, constants and parameters.
5. Interval	Time interval, on which you can perform manipulations.

Numeric data types and sub types

1. PLS_INTEGER or BINARY_INTEGER
   Signed integer in the range of -2,147,483,648 to 147,483,647.

2. BINARY_FLOAT
   Single-precision IEEE 754-format floating point number.

3. DOUBLE_FLOAT
   Double-precision IEEE 754-format floating point number.

4. NUMBER
   Fixed point or floating point number with absolute value in range 1E-103 to 1.Oe126.

BINARY_INTEGER is subtype of INTEGER and assigned values between - -2,147,483,647 to 2,147,483,647. It was the only indexing data type allowed for index-by tables before ora9i r2. PLS_INTEGER is subtype of BINARY_INTEGER again 2,147,483,647 to 2,147,483,647. PLS_INTEGER operations use machine arithmetic, so they are generally faster than NUMBER and INTEGER operations. BINARY_INTEGER and PLS_INTEGER are identical in Ora10g

PL/SQL character data types and subtypes

1. CHAR
   Fixed-length character string with maximum size of 32,767 bytes

2. VARCHAR2
   Variable-length character string with maximum size of 32,767 bytes

3. RAW
   Variable-length binary or byte string with maximum size of 32,767 bytes, not interpreted by PL/SQL

4. NCHAR
   Fixed-length national character string with maximum size of 32,767 bytes

5. NVARCHAR2
   Variable-length national character string with maximum size of 32,767 bytes

6. LONGFootref 1
   Variable-length character string with maximum size of 32,760 bytes

7. LONG RAWFootref 1
   Variable-length binary or byte string with maximum size of 32,760 bytes, not interpreted by PL/SQL

8. ROWIDFootref 1
   Physical row identifier, the address of a row in an ordinary table

9. UROWID   Universal row identifier (physical, logical, or foreign row identifier)

Predefined PL/SQL BOOLEAN data type

BOOLEAN data type is used to store logical values TRUE, FALSE or NULL. BOOLEAN variables, constants or parameters are declared by using the keyword BOOLEAN, as the following variable is declared of type BOOLEAN.

V_var BOOLEAN;

Note: SQL does not have BOOLEAN data type so it can't be used in SQL.

Variable declaration

Following example declares a variable of number type and in the executable section assigns 10 to it and simply prints it

Example

```
--Variable declaration
DECLARE
   v_var    NUMBER(2);
BEGIN
   v_var    := 10;
   DBMS_OUTPUT.put_line (v_var);
END;
/
Output
10
PL/SQL procedure successfully completed
```

Variable initialization

A variable can also be initialized at declaration time as following

```
--Variable initialization
DECLARE
   v_var    NUMBER(2):=10;
BEGIN
      DBMS_OUTPUT.put_line (v_var);
END;
/
Output
10
PL/SQL procedure successfully completed
```

Note: If length of a number variable is not given then it take 38 as default value unlike varchar2 in which length must be given, otherwise an error will rise at compile time.

Following example shows the use of BOOLEAN variable, the variable v_var is declared of type BOOLEAN then in the EXECUTABLE section value TRUE is assigned to v_var, at last in the IF statement it is checked that if the variable v_var contains TRUE then print the message.

Example

```
DECLARE
   v_var     BOOLEAN;
BEGIN
   v_var     := TRUE;

   IF v_var
   THEN
      DBMS_OUTPUT.put_line ('variable''s value is TRUE');
   END IF;
END;
/
Output
```
variable's value is TRUE
PL/SQL procedure successfully completed.

Scope of a PL/SQL variable

A variable declared in a block is called local to the block however global to the sub blocks, if a variable is declare in a block and same variable is declared in the sub block then both the variables will be in scope in the executable section of the sub block, however in sub block only the variable declared in that sub block will be visible, to reference the variable of outer block you have to qualify the variable's name with the name of the block (Block can have name by giving a label).
Variable cannot be referenced from two different blocks; variable declared in inner block cannot be referred in outer block;

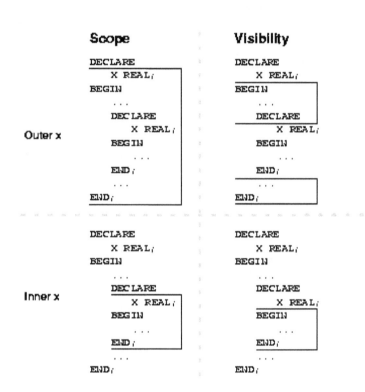

In the following example variable v_var is declared in outer block and a value 50 is assigned in the executable section and is printed in the inner block
Example 1

```
DECLARE
   v_var    NUMBER;
BEGIN
   v_var     := 50;

   BEGIN
      DBMS_OUTPUT.put_line (v_var);
   END;
END;
/
Output
50
PLSQL procedure successfully completed
```

In the following example Variable v_var is again declared in the inner block so print command will refer to that null variable

```
Example 2

DECLARE
   v_var    NUMBER;
BEGIN
   v_var     := 50;

   DECLARE
      v_var    NUMBER;
   BEGIN
      DBMS_OUTPUT.put_line (v_var);
   END;
END;
/
Output
PLSQL procedure successfully completed
```

When outer and inner block have same variable then you can label the outer block and can refer the outer block's variable in inner block by using label as following

```
Example 3

<<outer>>
DECLARE
   v_var    NUMBER;
BEGIN
   v_var      := 50;

   DECLARE
      v_var    NUMBER;
   BEGIN
      DBMS_OUTPUT.put_line (OUTER.v_var);
   END;
END;
/
Output
50
PLSQL procedure successfully completed
```

Implicit conversion

If a variable is declared as of varchar2 data type and a number value is assigned to it, oracle will implicitly convert number to varchar2 data type.
Similarly if a variable is declared as of number data type and a character value is assigned to it, it will implicitly convert character to number but the character value should consist on digits.
If a variable is declared of varchar2 data type then a date value can be assigned to it as implicit conversion will take place but a variable of type date can not accept character value until it is not in proper date format as explained in following examples

Example 1

Implicit conversion from number to character.

```
--Implicit conversion from number to character
DECLARE
   v_var   VARCHAR2 (10);
BEGIN
   v_var     := 56843;
   DBMS_OUTPUT.put_line (v_var);
END;
/
Output
56843
PL/SQL procedure successfully completed.
```

Implicit conversion from character to number.

```
--Implicit conversion from number to character
DECLARE
    v_var    NUMBER (10);
BEGIN
    v_var    := '56843';
    DBMS_OUTPUT.put_line (v_var);
END;
/
```
Output
```
56843
PL/SQL procedure successfully completed.
```

But if we try to assign no numeric data to the numeric variable then it will cause and error as following

```
--Implicit conversion from number to character
--Causes an error because a non numberic value is
--assigned to a number variable
DECLARE
    v_var    NUMBER (10);
BEGIN
    v_var    := '5684A';
    DBMS_OUTPUT.put_line (v_var);
END;
/
```
Output
```
DECLARE
*
ERROR at line 1:
ORA-06502: PL/SQL: numeric or value error: character to number conversion error
ORA-06512: at line 4
```

Implicit conversion from date to character

```
--Implicit conversion from date to character
DECLARE
    v_var    VARCHAR2(10);
BEGIN
    v_var    := SYSDATE;
    DBMS_OUTPUT.put_line (v_var);
END;
/
```
Output
```
16-JUL-09
PL/SQL procedure successfully completed.
```

Implicit conversion from character to date

```
--Implicit conversion from character to date
DECLARE
    v_var    date;
BEGIN
    v_var     := '01-JAN-2010';
    DBMS_OUTPUT.put_line (v_var);
END;
/
Output
01-JAN-10
PL/SQL procedure successfully completed.
```

Note: Conversion functions like TO_NUMBER, TO_CHAR and TO_DATE can also be used to perform explicit conversion like following

```
--Explicit conversion
DECLARE
    v_var    DATE;
BEGIN
                --Conversion function TO_DATE is used
    v_var     := TO_DATE ('01012010', 'DDMMRRRR');
    DBMS_OUTPUT.put_line (v_var);
END;
/
Output
01-JAN-10
PL/SQL procedure successfully completed.
```

Summary

In this chapter you have learned that a data type defines the format, constraints and valid range of values, PL/SQL data types can be categorized into scalar, composite, referenced and LOB, a variable is declared and initialized in declaration section and values within variable can be manipulated in executable section, a variable declared in the PL/SQL block is local to the block and global to the sub blocks.

You can assign a character value which consist on number digits to a number variable and implicit conversion takes place in this case, you can assign a number value to character variable and you can assign a date value to a character variable and vice versa.

Conversion function TO_CHAR, TO_NUMBER and TO_DATE are used to explicitly perform conversion.

Exercise

1. Create a program that accepts two values as input and adds subtracts divides and multiply them and print them.

2. What will be output and why?

```
--Varilble scope
DECLARE
   v_var1    NUMBER (4) := 2;
BEGIN
   DECLARE
      v_var1    NUMBER (4) := 4;
   BEGIN
      DBMS_OUTPUT.put_line (v_var1);
   END;
END;
/
```

3.   What is wrong with the following statement?

```
--label usage
DECLARE <<outer>>
   v_var1   NUMBER (4) := 2;
BEGIN
   DECLARE
      v_var1   NUMBER (4) := 4;
   BEGIN
      DBMS_OUTPUT.put_line (OUTER.v_var1);
   END;
END;
/
```

4.   What is wrong with the following statement

```
--The statement will generate and error
DECLARE
   v_num   NUMBER (4);
BEGIN
   v_num    := 56843;
   DBMS_OUTPUT.put_line (v_num);
END;
/
```

5.   An implicit conversion takes place in the following example when a character value '5684' is assigned to a NUMBER variable, what can you do to avoid this conversion?

```
--assigned to a number variable
DECLARE
   v_var   NUMBER (10);
BEGIN
   v_var    := '5684';
   DBMS_OUTPUT.put_line (v_var);
END;
/
```

4 INTERACTING WITH ORACLE SERVER

In this chapter you will learn about

How SQL statements are used in PL/SQL
SQL Select statement in PL/SQL block
SQL DML statements in PL/SQL block
Work with SQL attributes

How SQL statements are used in PL/SQL

SQL statements can be used in PL/SQL and can be sent to SQL engine for processing as one block at one time.

SELECT statement in PL/SQL

SELECT statement that returns one row can be used in PL/SQL block with additional INTO clause, INTO clause is used to hold the value returned by the SELECT statement.
SELECT statement that returns more than one row raises an error, to process multiple rows in PL/SQL CURSORs are used which are covered in a coming lesson.
SELECT statement that returns no row also raises an error.

The following example uses SELECT statement in PL/SQL block, two variables are declared to take the returned values of EMPNO and ENAME into the INTO clause and then printed through DBMS_OUTPUT.PUT_LINE procedure.
Note that the variable should be of the same data type as the returned column and should be in the same order as columns in the SELECT statement, For example you cannot write "V_ENAME , V_EMPNO" in the INTO clause because the columns in the SELECT statement are not in this order so the columns should be as "V_EMPNO, V_ENAME".

Example 1

```
--SELECT statement in PL/SQL block
DECLARE
    v_empno    NUMBER;
    v_ename    VARCHAR2 (30);
BEGIN
    SELECT empno,
           ename
    INTO   v_empno,
           v_ename
    FROM   emp
    WHERE  empno = 7900;

    DBMS_OUTPUT.put_line (v_ename);
END;
/
Output
JAMES
PL/SQL procedure successfully completed
```

The error (NO_DATA_FOUND) will rise if the SELECT statement will not return a row as following

Example 2

```
--SELECT statement in PL/SQL block
DECLARE
    v_empno    NUMBER;
    v_ename    VARCHAR2 (30);
BEGIN
    SELECT empno,
           ename
    INTO   v_empno,
           v_ename
    FROM   emp
    WHERE  empno = 1144;

    DBMS_OUTPUT.put_line (v_ename);
END;
/
Output
declare
*
```

ERROR at line 1:
ORA-01403: no data found
ORA-06512: at line 5

If more than one row is selected then also an error comes as in the following example

Example 3

```
--SELECT statement in PL/SQL block, WHERE clause is commented to select more than
one row
DECLARE
    v_empno    NUMBER;
    v_ename    VARCHAR2 (30);
BEGIN
    SELECT empno,
           ename
    INTO   v_empno,
           v_ename
    FROM   emp;
--    WHERE  empno = 7900;

    DBMS_OUTPUT.put_line (v_ename);
END;
/
Output
declare
*
ERROR at line 1:
ORA-01422: exact fetch returns more than requested number of rows
ORA-06512: at line 5
PL/SQL procedure successfully completed
```

It means SELECT statement used in PL/SQL block should return only one row.

DML statements in PL/SQL

DML STATEMENTS in PL/SQL can be used, unlike SELECT statements no error raises when DML statements affect no row or more than one row, you can use SQL Attributes to know the effect of DML statement in PL/SQL.
The following statement is used to update EMP table, SQL Attribute %ROWCOUNT is used to identify the number of records updated.

Example 1

```
--Update statement inside PL/SQL
BEGIN
    UPDATE emp
    SET job = 'ANALYST'
    WHERE   empno = 7698;

    DBMS_OUTPUT.put_line (SQL%ROWCOUNT || ' Record updated');
END;
/
Output
```
1 Rows updated
PL/SQL procedure successfully completed.
The following statement is used to Delete a record from emp table, Note the that SQL%FOUND
attribute is used.

Example 2

```
--Delete statement with PL/SQL block
BEGIN
    DELETE FROM emp
    WHERE          empno = 7900;

    IF SQL%FOUND
    THEN
        DBMS_OUTPUT.put_line (SQL%ROWCOUNT || ' Rows updated');
    END IF;
END;
/
Output
```
1 Rows updated
PL/SQL procedure successfully completed.

In the following example the EMP table is updated for a nonexistent EMP, note that no error raised
unlike SELECT statement.

Example 3

```
--Update statement inside PL/SQL
BEGIN
    UPDATE emp
    SET job = 'ANALYST'
    WHERE  empno = 7698;

    DBMS_OUTPUT.put_line (SQL%ROWCOUNT || ' Record updated');
END;
/
Output
```
0 Rows updated
PL/SQL procedure successfully completed.

SQL Attributes

SQL attributes are used to identify the most recent rows that are affected by DML SQL statements. You must have studied about SQL Attributes, it is just a remainder.
Following four types of SQL attributes are used

%FOUND
Returns TRUE when the most recent SQL statement have effected any row (in DML operation) or SELECT statement have returned one or more rows and FALSE otherwise.

%NOTFOUND
Return TRUE when the most recent SQL statement has not affected any row and FALSE otherwise, it is just an opposite of %FOUND.

%ROWCOUND
Return the number of rows affected by the most recent SQL statement.

%ISOPEN
Always returns FALSE because SQL statement closes the cursor immediately after execution.

Summary

In this chapter you have learned how SQL statements (SELECT, INSERT, UPDATE, DELETE) are used within PL/SQL block, To be used in PL/SQL SQL select statement must return one and only one row otherwise the exception NO_DATA_FOUND or TOO_MANY_ROWS will return, SQL attributes are used to know the effect of DML statements in PL/SQL.

Exercise

1. Write SELECT statements inside PL/SQL block and get EMPNO, ENAME, job and mgr columns of EMP table for any particular employee and print it.

2. Write an update statement inside PL/SQL block that will show a message "Record does not exist" when no record is updated, the code should update the record when the record exists.

5 CONDICTIONAL CONTROL STATEMENTS

In this chapter you will learn about

Conditional control statements
IF-THEN structure
IF-THEN-ELSE structure
IF-THEN-ELSIF structure
Nested IF statements

Conditional control statements

Conditional control is a term that is used to describe the way program flow diverges, depending on certain condition(s). We use conditional control statements by referring keywords IF-THEN-ELSE which are very close to formal language.

IF-THEN Structure

IF-THEN Statement can be divided into three types

1 IF-THEN
2 IF-THEN-ELSE
3 IF-THEN-ELSIF-ELSE

IF-THEN

The basic type of conditional control is IF-THEN Statement

Syntax

```
        IF Condition THEN
            Statement 1
            Statement 2
            ..............
        END IF;
```
Condition should be true to execute the statements after THEN keyword. Condition is made by using compression operators like =, <, <=,>, >=, Like, Between, IN.

Example 1

```
BEGIN
    IF 1 > 0
    THEN
        DBMS_OUTPUT.put_line ('1 is greater than 0');
    END IF;
END;
/
```

The output

1 is greater than 0
PL/SQL procedure successfully completed.

Because 1>0 yields TRUE so the DBMS_OUTPUT.PUT_LINE executes and prints the output.
Note: that the Statements between THEN and END IF are executed if the condition in IF clause is TRUE.

Similarly if you write

Example 2

```
BEGIN
    IF 1 < 0
    THEN
        DBMS_OUTPUT.put_line ('1 is less than 0');
    END IF;
END;
/
```
The output
PL/SQL procedure successfully completed.

Because the 1<0 yields FLASE so the DBMS_OUTPUT.PUT_LINE does not execute, though the Procedure executes successfully.

IF-THEN-ELSE

Syntax

```
        IF CONDICTION THEN
           Statement 1;
           Statement 2;
           ................
        ELSE
           Statement 1;
           Statement 2;
        END IF;
```

This type of IF Statements have an extra keyword ELSE, If the condition of first IF does not yield TRUE then statements in the ELSE clause gets executed.

Example 1

```
BEGIN
   IF 1 < 0
   THEN
      DBMS_OUTPUT.put_line ('1 is less than 0');
   ELSE
      DBMS_OUTPUT.put_line ('1 is Greater than 0');
   END IF;
END;
/
```
Output
1 is Greater than 0
PL/SQL procedure successfully completed.

Because the 1<0 yields FLASE so the DBMS_OUTPUT.PUT_LINE does not execute for the first Statement but executes the statement in ELSE clause.
Similarly if the condition yields TRUE then the first statement executes as shown below

Example 2

```
BEGIN
    IF 1 > 0
    THEN
        DBMS_OUTPUT.put_line ('1 is Greater than 0');
    ELSE
        DBMS_OUTPUT.put_line ('1 is less than 0');
    END IF;
END;
/
```
Output

1 is Greater than 0

PL/SQL procedure successfully completed.

Note: that only statements in IF or Statements in ELSE clause are executed.

IF-THEN-ELSIF

Syntax

IF CONDICTION THEN
        Statement 1;
        Statement 2;

        ....

ELSIF CONDICTION THEN
        Statement 1;
        Statement 2;

        ....

ELSIF CONDICTION THEN
        Statement 1;
        Statement 2;

        ....

ELSE
        Statement 1;
        Statement 2;

        ....

END IF;

In this type of IF STATEMENT an extra clause ELSIF is needed ,If the first condition yields FLASE then second condition in ELSIF is checked and STATEMENT within it are executed if the CONDICTION yields TRUE.

At last an ELSE clause can also be added which will ensure that if all the condictions of IF and ELSIF got FALSE then statements within ELSE clause will defiantly execute.

Example 1

```
BEGIN
   IF 1 < 0
   THEN
      DBMS_OUTPUT.put_line ('1 is less than 0');
   ELSIF 1 > 0
   THEN
      DBMS_OUTPUT.put_line ('1 is Greater than 0');
   END IF;
END;
/
```

Output
1 is Greater than 0
PL/SQL procedure successfully completed.

The first IF condition yields FLASE so the second ELSIF condition is checked because it yields TRUE so the statement within it is executed. If the second statement also yields FALSE then no output comes.

Example 2

```
BEGIN
   IF 1 < 0
   THEN
      DBMS_OUTPUT.put_line ('1 is less than 0');
   ELSIF 1 > 2
   THEN
      DBMS_OUTPUT.put_line ('1 is Greater than 2');
   END IF;
END;
/
```

Output
PL/SQL procedure successfully completed.

No output, because 1 can never be less than 0 and 1 can never be greater than 2.

Example 3

```
BEGIN
   IF TO_CHAR (SYSDATE, 'DY') IN ('SAT', 'SUN')
   THEN
      DBMS_OUTPUT.put_line ('Today is off day');
   ELSIF TO_CHAR (SYSDATE, 'DY') IN ('MON', 'TUE', 'WED', 'THU', 'FRI')
   THEN
      DBMS_OUTPUT.put_line ('Today is working day');
   END IF;
END;
/

Output
Today is off day
PL/SQL procedure successfully completed.
```

The IF CONDICTIONS in above example check that either it is working day or holiday and print the result accordingly. The result can be different according to the day.
ELSE clause can also be used as last clause so that if all conditions yield FLASE then ELSE gets executed.
Use of ELSE clause ensures that the STATEMENTS within it are executed if no other IF or ELSIF condition gets true.

Example 4

```
BEGIN
   IF 1 < 0
   THEN
      DBMS_OUTPUT.put_line ('1 is less than 0');
   ELSIF 1 > 2
   THEN
      DBMS_OUTPUT.put_line ('1 is Greater than 2');
   ELSE
      DBMS_OUTPUT.put_line
                      ('1 is neither less than 0 nor greater than 2');
   END IF;
END;
/

Output

1 is neither less than 0 nor greater then 2
PL/SQL procedure successfully completed.
```

NOTE: The keyword is ELSIF not ELSEIF

There can be multiple ELSIF statements

Example 5

```
BEGIN
   IF 1 < 0
   THEN
      DBMS_OUTPUT.put_line ('1 is less than 0');
   ELSIF 1 > 2
   THEN
      DBMS_OUTPUT.put_line ('1 is Greater than 2');
   ELSIF 2 > 3
   THEN
      DBMS_OUTPUT.put_line ('2 is Greater than 3');
   ELSIF 3 > 2
   THEN
      DBMS_OUTPUT.put_line ('3 is Greater than 2');
   ELSIF 4 < 5
   THEN
      DBMS_OUTPUT.put_line ('4 is less than 5');
   ELSE
      DBMS_OUTPUT.put_line
                     ('1 is neither less than 0 nor greater than 2');
   END IF;
END;
/
```

Output

```
3 is Greater than 2
PL/SQL procedure successfully completed.
```

The third ELSIF 3>2 yields TRUE so the statement within it executes,
As soon as any condition yields true the statements within it are executed and all other ELSIF and ELSE clauses are ignored as the forth condition ELSIF 4<5 also yields true in above example but it is ignored because the condition above yields true.
This means that STATEMENTS within only one condition can be executed at one time and upper conditions gets priority because they are executed first.

Compound IF Conditions

Logical operators (AND, OR, NOT) are used to make an IF CONDICTION compound.

Example 1

```
BEGIN
    IF 1 > 0 AND 1 < 2
    THEN
        DBMS_OUTPUT.put_line ('1 is greater than 0 and less than 2');
    END IF;
END;
/
```

OUTPUT

```
1 is greater than 0 and less then 2
PL/SQL procedure successfully completed.
```

Note: In some cases the condition yields NULL instead of TRUE or FLASE, If any condition yields NULL then it is similar as FALSE.

Example 2

```
BEGIN
    IF 1 = NULL
    THEN
        DBMS_OUTPUT.put_line ('1 is equal to null');
    ELSE
        DBMS_OUTPUT.put_line ('Any condition involves NULL returns NULL');
    END IF;
END;
/
```

Output

Any condition involves NULL returns NULL
PL/SQL procedure successfully completed.

Because NULL cannot be compared to anything, any condition compared to NULL returns NULL so first condition is ignored.

NESTED IF Statements

IF statements can be nested

Example 1

```
BEGIN
    IF TO_CHAR (SYSDATE, 'DY') IN ('SAT', 'SUN')
    THEN
        IF TO_CHAR (SYSDATE, 'dd') <= 7
        THEN
            DBMS_OUTPUT.put_line ('Today is off day and first week of the month');
        ELSE
            DBMS_OUTPUT.put_line ('Today is off day but not first week of the
month');
        END IF;
    END IF;
END;
/
```

The first CONDICTION checks the day, If it is Saturday or Sunday then the second CONDITION checks that either it is first week of month or not , the message is printed accordingly.
There is no limit to nest the IF Statements until your ability to handle complexity.

Note: The above example depends on the day of the week, you can change the date so that it returns Saturday or Sunday in IF CONDICTION for checking purpose.

Summary

In this chapter you have learned about Conditional control statements that are used to make decisions in PL/SQL, You have learned about IF-THEN, IF-THEN-ELSE and IF-THEN-ELSIF structure. You have learned how to make successive decisions by using NESTED IF statements and that there is no limit to nesting IF statements.

Exercise

1. Write a simple if statement to check the year if it is 2009 then print "The year is 2009"

2. Write a if statement to check the year if it is 2009 then print "The year is 2009" else
   Print "The year is not 2009"

3. Declare a variable V_MARKS as number and make it as substation variable to get the
   Value at run time. In the Executable section check if the variable's value is greater than 100
   then show the message "Invalid Number" else if the variable's value is less than or equal to
   100 and greater than or equal 80 then show the message "A One Grade" else if variable's
   value is less than 80 and greater than or equal 70 then show the message "A Grade" else if the
   variables value is less than 70 and greater than or equal 60 then show the Message "B Grade"
   else if variable's value is less than 60 and Greater than 0 then show the message "Fail" else
   the value can be negative only so show the message "Invalid Value".
   Run the code by giving it different values.

4. Write a program that should accept any two numbers and a symbol (+, -, *, /), the two
   numbers should be added, subtracted, multiplied or divided according to user input and result
   should be shown.
   Hint: use substitution variables to get the input.

5. What is wrong with the following program?

```
DECLARE
    v_num1          NUMBER (8)    := &number1;
    v_num2          NUMBER (8)    := &number2;
    v_symbol        VARCHAR2 (1)  := '&symbol';
    v_calculation   NUMBER (8);
BEGIN
    IF v_symbol = '+'
    THEN
        v_calculation    := v_num1 + v_num2;
    ELSEIF v_symbol = '-'
    THEN
        v_calculation    := v_num1 - v_num2;
    END IF;

    DBMS_OUTPUT.put_line (v_calculation);
END;
/
```

6 ITERATIVE LOOP STRUCTURES

In this chapter you will learn about

What is a loop?
Simple loop
For Loop
While loop
Nested loop

What is a loop?

Loop is used for the repetition of statements. For example use following loop if you want to print 'Farhan' hundred times or simply want to print numbers from 1 to 100.

Example 1

```
--prints 'Farhan' hundred times
BEGIN
    FOR i IN 1 .. 100
    LOOP
        DBMS_OUTPUT.put_line ('Farhan');
    END LOOP;
END;
/

Output
'Farhan' Will be printed hundred times

Example 2

--prints numbers from one to hundred
BEGIN
    FOR i IN 1 .. 100
    LOOP
        DBMS_OUTPUT.put_line (i);
    END LOOP;
END;
/
Output
Number will be printed from 1 to 100 like
1
2
3......
```

Types of Loop

1. Simple Loop
2. For Loop
3. While Loop

1. Simple Loop

Syntax

```
LOOP
STATEMENT 1
STATEMENT 2
……………….
EXIT WHEN condition
END LOOP;
```

Simple loop Starts with Keyword LOOP and ends with keyword END LOOP.
EXIT WHEN clause is used to terminate the loop, until EXIT WHEN clause does not terminates, the STATEMENT within loop continue to repeat. A condition is used inside EXIT WHEN clause, which needs to be TRUE to exit the loop successfully, simple loop, continues to execute if EXIT clause is not used.

For example the following loop will continue to print numbers until it reaches 50.
After reaching 50 the EXIT WHEN clause return TRUE and loop terminates. To keep track the repetition number, a variable is needed, which is initialized to 1 and is incremented by 1 in the each iteration of the loop. In EXIT WHEN condition the counter is used to check that either the loop is repeated 50 times or not.

Example 1

```
--Prints numbers from 1 to 50
DECLARE
   v_number    NUMBER := 1;
BEGIN
   LOOP
      DBMS_OUTPUT.put_line (v_number);
      EXIT WHEN v_number = 50;
      v_number      := v_number + 1;
   END LOOP;
END;
/
OUTPUT
--Prints numbers from 1 to 50
```

The following example prints the table of 5. IF Condition is used to check that either the counter is equal to 10 or not, it is an alternative to write the condition inside EXIT clause.

```
Example 2

DECLARE
    v_number    NUMBER := 1;
BEGIN
    LOOP
        DBMS_OUTPUT.put_line ('5 * ' || v_number || '=' || 5 * v_number);

        IF v_number = 10
        THEN
            EXIT;
        END IF;
          /*The above condition can also be written as
            EXIT WHEN v_number=10*/

        v_number        := v_number + 1;
    END LOOP;
END;
    /

Output
```
5 * 1=5
5 * 2=10
5 * 3=15
5 * 4=20
5 * 5=25
5 * 6=30
5 * 7=35
5 * 8=40
5 * 9=45
5 * 10=50

PL/SQL procedure successfully completed.

2. For Loop

This is most widely used type of loop.
In this loop it is defined in the header of the loop that how many time the loop will execute.

Syntax

```
FOR COUNTER IN [REVERSE] Lower_limit..Upper_limit LOOP
STATEMENT 1;
STATEMENT 2;
……………...
……………...
END LOOP;
```

A COUNTER is an identifier which contains the current iteration number of the loop; it can be referred in the STATEMETS inside loop.
The Lower_limit defines the starting value and Upper_limit defines the ending value of a loop. If Lower limit's value is 1 and Upper_limit's value is 10 then loop will execute 10 times from 1 to 10.
REVERSE Keyword forces the loop to execute in reverse.

A simple example below prints numbers from 1 to 50.

Example 1

```
--Prints numbers from 1 to 50
BEGIN
   FOR i IN 1 .. 50
   LOOP
      DBMS_OUTPUT.put_line (i);
   END LOOP;
END;
/

OUTPUT
--Prints numbers from 1 to 50
```

Following example prints coming 25 days and identifies holidays.

Example 2

```
DECLARE
   v_date    DATE := SYSDATE;
BEGIN
   FOR i IN 1 .. 25
   LOOP
      IF TO_CHAR (v_date, 'DY') = 'SUN'
      THEN
         DBMS_OUTPUT.put_line (TO_CHAR (v_date, 'DAY dd MONTH') || ' HOLIDAY');
      ELSE
         DBMS_OUTPUT.put_line (TO_CHAR (v_date, 'DAY dd MONTH'));
      END IF;

      v_date      := v_date + 1;
   END LOOP;
END;
/
```

Output

```
MONDAY    11 MAY
TUESDAY   12 MAY
WEDNESDAY 13 MAY
THURSDAY  14 MAY
FRIDAY    15 MAY
SATURDAY  16 MAY
SUNDAY    17 MAY     HOLIDAY
```
....
PL/SQL procedure successfully completed.

Following example is used to execute the loop in reverse.
Note that only REVERSE keyword is used and there is no change of the ordering in the lower and upper limits.

Example 3

```
--Loop executes in Reverse
--only REVERSE keyword is additional
DECLARE
   v_date   DATE := SYSDATE;
BEGIN
   FOR i IN REVERSE 1 .. 5
   LOOP
      DBMS_OUTPUT.put_line (i);
   END LOOP;
END;
/
Output
5
4
3
2
1
PL/SQL procedure successfully completed.
```

Note: Lower limit can never be greater than upper limit else Loop will not execute.

3. While Loop

While loop is similar to simple loop, the only difference is that in while loop EXIT Condition is in the header of Loop and it is checked in the starting. Loop executes only if the CONDICTION returns TRUE.

Syntax

WHILE CONDICTION=TRUE LOOP
 STATEMENT 1;
 STATEMENT 2;
………………….
END LOOP;

Following example is same that was used with simple loop, the only difference is that the condition for exiting the loop is checked in the header.

Example 1

```
DECLARE
    v_number    NUMBER := 1;
BEGIN
    WHILE v_number <= 10/*Loop terminates when this condition return FLASE*/
    LOOP
        DBMS_OUTPUT.put_line ('5 * ' || v_number || '=' || 5 * v_number);
        v_number      := v_number + 1;
    END LOOP;
END;
/

Output
5 * 1=5
5 * 2=10
5 * 3=15
5 * 4=20
5 * 5=25
5 * 6=30
5 * 7=35
5 * 8=40
5 * 9=45
5 * 10=50
```
PL/SQL procedure successfully completed.

4. Nested Loop

You can nest one loop (inner loop) inside another loop (outer loop), the inner loop executes completely for the each iteration of outer loop. The following example uses nested loop , the outer loop executes 2 times, the inner loop executes 10 time for each iteration of outer loop so inner loop executes 2*10=20 times.

Example 1

```
--Nested loop
BEGIN
    FOR i IN 1 .. 2 LOOP          --Outer loop
        FOR j IN 1 .. 10 LOOP     --Inner loop
            DBMS_OUTPUT.put_line (   'outer''s iteration='|| i|| ' inner''s
iteration='|| j);
        END LOOP;
    END LOOP;
END;
/
```

Output
outer's iteration=1 inner's iteration=1
outer's iteration=1 inner's iteration=2
outer's iteration=1 inner's iteration=3
outer's iteration=1 inner's iteration=4
outer's iteration=1 inner's iteration=5
outer's iteration=1 inner's iteration=6
outer's iteration=1 inner's iteration=7
outer's iteration=1 inner's iteration=8
outer's iteration=1 inner's iteration=9
outer's iteration=1 inner's iteration=10
outer's iteration=2 inner's iteration=1
outer's iteration=2 inner's iteration=2
outer's iteration=2 inner's iteration=3
outer's iteration=2 inner's iteration=4
outer's iteration=2 inner's iteration=5
outer's iteration=2 inner's iteration=6
outer's iteration=2 inner's iteration=7
outer's iteration=2 inner's iteration=8
outer's iteration=2 inner's iteration=9
outer's iteration=2 inner's iteration=10
PL/SQL procedure successfully completed.

The following example prints the table of 5, 6, 7, 8, 9 and 10.

Example 2

```
BEGIN
    FOR i IN 5 .. 10
    LOOP
        FOR j IN 1 .. 10
        LOOP
            DBMS_OUTPUT.put_line (i || ' * ' || j || ' = ' || i * j);
        END LOOP;
    END LOOP;
END;

Output
--Tables of 5,6,7,8,9 and 10
```

5. The CONTINUE condition

The CONTINUE condition is introduced in oracle 11g, The CONTINUE condition is used to terminate a specific iteration or part of an iteration (Statements). It is used in a similar way as EXIT condition is used, the difference is that Exit statement terminates the loop while the CONTINUE condition terminates an iteration or part of an iteration (Statements).
CONTINUE condition can be used with all types of Loops.

Syntax

```
LOOP
CONTINUE WHEN condiction;
STATEMENT 1;
STATEMENT 2;
………………...
END LOOP;
```

The following example uses CONTINUE condition, when the (i/2)=0 means when the number will be 2,4,6,8 or 10 the CONTINUE condition terminates the iteration and control pass to the next iteration.

Note: CONTINUE condition can only terminate the STATEMENTS coming after it , the STATEMENTS before it are executed.

Example 1

```
--Use of continue condition
BEGIN
    FOR i IN 1 .. 10
    LOOP
        CONTINUE WHEN (i/2)=0;
            /* The above condition can also be written as
            IF (I/2)=0 THEN
            CONTINUE;
            END IF*/
        DBMS_OUTPUT.put_line (i);
    END LOOP;
END;

Output
1
3
5
7
9
```

Summary

In this chapter you have learned about iterative control structure called loop that is used to repeat a statement or statements multiple times, there are three loop structures that are used in PL/SQL as Simple loop, For loop and While loop. Loop can be nested; there is no limit to nesting loop but your ability to handle the complexity.
CONTINUE statement is used to ignore a complete iteration or part of iteration of a loop.

Exercise

1. Write a SIMPLE LOOP, a FOR LOOP and a WHILE LOOP to print 'LOOP   EXAMPLE' 50 times;

2. Write a loop that should print holidays of the year 2009

3. Write a loop that should print holidays of the year 2009 by using continue condition.

4. Write a program that should print holidays of three year 2009, 2010 and 2011 by using a nested loop.

5. What's wrong with the following program?

```
BEGIN
    FOR i IN 1 .. 50
    LOOP
        DBMS_OUTPUT.put_line (i);
END;
/
```

7　PL/SQL COMPOSITE DATA TYPES

In this chapter you will learn about

Introduction to composite data type
What are records?
%ROWTYPE records
User defined records

What are Records?

Records are similar as a row of a table, Records are used for temporary storage of data, because records are local to PL/SQL so they boost performance, Records can be alternative to a large number of variables, records can be declared by using %ROWTYPE that are based on a table or on a cursor, means the structure of the record will be similar to that of a table or cursor's record and if the table or cursor changes later on the record will be automatically changed.

There are two types of records

1 %ROWTYPE Record
2 User defined Record

1.　%ROWTYPE Record

Syntax

Record_name Table|Cursor%ROWTYPE;

%ROWTYPE records are declared by using the above syntax; these can be based on a table or cursor. Following example declares a record by using %ROWTYPE, the record is based on EMP table so it has similar structure as a row of EMP table, Because structure of EMP_REC is similar to that of EMP row so values can be selected in it directly from EMP table.
To refer any field in the record dot notation is used as EMP_REC.EMPNO, field names are similar as that of columns names in the EMP table, only three fields are referred in following example though you can try all.
Cursor based records are covered in the coming lessons.

Example 1

```
DECLARE
    emp_rec    emp%ROWTYPE;
BEGIN
    SELECT *
    INTO    emp_rec
    FROM    emp
    WHERE   empno = 7900;

    DBMS_OUTPUT.put_line (    emp_rec.empno
                          || ' '
                          || emp_rec.ename
                          || ' '
                          || emp_rec.sal
                          );
END;
/
Output
```
7900 JAMES 1000
PL/SQL procedure successfully completed.

2. User defined Record

Syntax

TYPE type_name IS RECORD(field1 datatype1 | %TYPE[NOT NULL] [:=default value],
                         Field2 datatype2 | %TYPE[NOT NULL] [:=default value],
                         ....|
%ROWTYPE);
Record_name type_name;

User defined record is declared when a user want to defined his own fields in the record.
Type indicates that some composite data types is going to generate, TYPE_NAME is the name of the
type that can be any meaningful name up to 30 characters, IS RECORD identifies that the record is
going to generate, fild1 identifies the fields name, data type indicates its data type or %ROWTYPE
can also be used, NOT NULL ensures that the particular field cannot be null, Assignment operator is
used to give an initial value to the field, %ROWTYPE can also be used to get all the fields of table,
and at last RECORD_NAME declares a record variable based on the declared record type.
Fields declaration inside record type is similar to that of columns declaration in the table.
The following statement creates a type EMP_TY with two fields ID and NAME and declares a record
based on the record type.

Example 1

```
DECLARE
    TYPE emp_ty IS RECORD (
        ID      NUMBER,
        NAME    VARCHAR2 (20)
    );

    emp_tb    emp_ty;
BEGIN
    emp_tb.ID       := 1;
    emp_tb.NAME     := 'FARHAN';
    DBMS_OUTPUT.put_line (emp_tb.ID || ' ' || emp_tb.NAME);
END;
/
Output
1 FARHAN
PL/SQL procedure successfully completed.
```

The following example shows the use of default value, the default value 'FARHAN' is given to NAME field so though in the Executable section not any value is given to NAME field in spite we get the default value as output.

Example 2

```
DECLARE
    TYPE emp_ty IS RECORD (
        ID      NUMBER,
        NAME    VARCHAR2 (20) := 'FARHAN'
    );

    emp_tb    emp_ty;
BEGIN
    emp_tb.ID    := 1;
    DBMS_OUTPUT.put_line (emp_tb.ID || ' ' || emp_tb.NAME);
END;
/
Output
1 FARHAN
PL/SQL procedure successfully completed.
```

Note: that field declared as NOT NULL must be given a default value.

Summary

In this chapter you have learned about the PL/SQL records, PL/SQL records are an alternative of declaring lots of variables and processing is much faster because they are local to the PL/SQL, %ROWTYPE records are based on a table or cursor and their structure is similar to the row of a table or cursor, user defined records are declared if the employee wants to have his own fields in the record.

Exercise

1. Declare a record that should hold an entire row of dept table and print a complete row of dept table.

2. Declare a record to hold a row of fields' EMPNO, ENAME, DEPTNO, DNAME from EMP and dept table, join the tables and get the row for one particular employs.

8 PL/SQL COMPOSITE DATA TYPES

In this chapter you will learn about

What are PLSQL collections?
Associative array
Nested tables
VRRAYs

What are PLSQL collections?

PLSQL collections are just like tables but collections can only store data temporarily when declared in PL/SQL though some Collections can be created in SQL that can store data permanently, which are covered in a coming lesson 'Oracle object types'. Collections are local to the PLSQL blocks hence they boost the performance; Complex calculations can be performed by using collections.

Note: that terms PLSQL table, Nested tables and Arrays all refer to collections.

Collections are of following three types

1 Associative array
2 Nested table
3 Varry
Nested tables and Varrys can also be declared at database level through SQL which are covered in a coming lesson.

1. Associative Array

Syntax

TYPE type_name IS TABLE OF datatype
INDEX BY BINARY_INTEGER;

Table_name type_name;

Associative arrays are used to store data temporarily for performing complex calculations.
In the syntax TYPE indicates that it is a type that is going to generate, type_name specifies the name
of the type, IS TABLE OF indicates that table type is going to generate, data type shows any valid
data type (certain data type are not allowed in collections but are out of this book's scope), INDEX
BY BINARY_INTEGER is used to assign sequence numbers (indexes) to array as similar in arrays
of C. BINARY_INTEGER or PLS_INTEGER both data types can be used for indexing as both are
similar after 10g. After declaring table type you declare variable of that type so that you can refer
table variable as normal variable.
Following example creates a table type COUNT_TY and a table variable COUNT_TAB.
Whenever a value is assigned to a PLSQL table the position is also specified,

COUNT_TAB(1):=100;

The above statement specifies that value 100 is assigned to COUNT_TAB at index position 1, to get
the value of index 1 into variable V_VARIABLE following syntax is used

V_variable:=count_tab(1);

So in the following example first loop executes 10 times and assigns 10 values to associative array COUNT_TAB and second loop executes 10 times to get the values of the array COUNT_TAB

```
Example 1

DECLARE
    -- A table type is declared first
    TYPE count_ty IS TABLE OF NUMBER
        INDEX BY BINARY_INTEGER;

    -- A variable is then declared of the above table type
    count_tab    count_ty;
BEGIN
    --Loop assigns 10 values at the same position as the index number
    FOR i IN 1 .. 10
    LOOP
        count_tab (i)     := i;
    END LOOP;
-- loop to get the values of table count_tab
    FOR i IN 1 .. 10
    LOOP
        DBMS_OUTPUT.put_line (count_tab (i));
    END LOOP;
END;
/
Output
1
2
3
4
5
6
7
8
9
10
PL/SQL procedure successfully completed.
```

The following example finds duplicate values in the associative array, In the example two arrays are defined based on same type, 10 values are assigned to array count_tab and value 8 is assigned to 9th index so index 8 and 9 both have value 8 so 8 is a duplicate value. To find the duplicate value the whole array is assigned to other array count_tab2(assigning one PL/SQL table to other became possible in oracle 10g).

Now one loop is executed from 1 to 10 by referring count_tab2.FIRST .. count_tab2.LAST, FIRST and LAST are methods which refer to first and last elements of the array. For each element of outer loop the whole inner loop will execute putting 1 increment for each matched element between outer loop and inner loop. As soon as a duplicate value come the counter V_COUNT becomes 2 and the statement becomes true to terminate the loop. After complete iteration of inner loop the count V_COUT is set to 0 so that it can be started from 0 with each new element of outer loop.

Example 2

```
DECLARE
    TYPE count_ty IS TABLE OF NUMBER
        INDEX BY BINARY_INTEGER;

    count_tab      count_ty;
    count_tab2     count_ty;
    v_count        NUMBER;
BEGIN
    FOR i IN 1 .. 10
    LOOP
        count_tab (i)      := i;
    END LOOP;

    count_tab (9)      := 8;
    count_tab2         := count_tab;

    FOR i IN count_tab2.FIRST .. count_tab2.LAST
    LOOP
        v_count      := 0;
        DBMS_OUTPUT.put_line (i || ' I');

        FOR j IN count_tab.FIRST .. count_tab.LAST
        LOOP
            DBMS_OUTPUT.put_line (j || ' J');

            IF count_tab2 (i) = count_tab (j)
            THEN
                v_count      := v_count + 1;
            END IF;

            IF v_count > 1
            THEN
                raise_application_error (-20050,
                                    count_tab2 (i) || ' is a duplicate value'
                                    );
            END IF;
        END LOOP;
    END LOOP; END; /
```

```
Output
10 J
8 I
1 J
```

```
2 J
3 J
4 J
5 J
6 J
7 J
8 J
9 J
DECLARE
*
ERROR at line 1:
ORA-20050: 8 is a duplicate value
ORA-06512: at line 27
```

2. Two Dimensional Associative Arrays

Syntax

TYPE type_name IS TABLE OF Record_type
INDEX BY BINARY_INTEGER;

Table_name type_name;

Two dimensional associative arrays are similar to one dimensional associative array except that two dimensional arrays have more than one columns, Syntax for creating two dimensional arrays is similar to one dimensional arrays except that in two dimensional arrays a Record_type(user defined or %ROWTYPE) is used instead of a data type so columns in the two dimensional arrays are referred by their name. To refer any specific column a dot notation is used as following

To assign a value to the two dimensional array's column the following syntax is used

        Table(index).column:=value;

To get a value from two dimensional array's column into variable V_VAR following syntax is used

        V_var:=table(index).column;

The following example creates a two dimensional array with columns ID and NAME, User defined record EMP_REC is created with two columns ID and NAME and record type is assigned to table type EMP_TY so the table type EMP_TY can have two columns ID and NAME.

All other processing is similar to that of one dimensional array, Values are assigned to emp_tb's colums ID and NAME at three indexes and printed at last.

Not that CHR(10) is carriage return used for new line.

Example 1

```
DECLARE
    TYPE emp_rec IS RECORD (
        ID      NUMBER,
        NAME    VARCHAR2 (20)
    );

    TYPE emp_ty IS TABLE OF emp_rec
        INDEX BY BINARY_INTEGER;

    emp_tb    emp_ty;
BEGIN
    emp_tb (1).ID      := 1;
    emp_tb (1).NAME    := 'FARHAN';
    --------------
    emp_tb (2).ID      := 2;
    emp_tb (2).NAME    := 'ALI';
    --------------
    emp_tb (3).ID      := 3;
    emp_tb (3).NAME    := 'WAQAR';
    --------------
    DBMS_OUTPUT.put_line (   emp_tb (1).ID
                          || ' '
                          || emp_tb (1).NAME
                          || CHR (10)
                          || emp_tb (2).ID
                          || ' '
                          || emp_tb (2).NAME
                          || CHR (10)
                          || emp_tb (3).ID
                          || ' '
                          || emp_tb (3).NAME
                         );
END;
/
Output
1 FARHAN
2 ALI
PL/SQL procedure successfully completed.
```

Following example shows the use of %ROWTYPE records, table type EMP_TY have the record type emp%ROWTYPE so it have all the columns of EMP table, In the executable section first loop executes 10 times and assigns some values to each column of EMP_TB, Same values are assigned to all columns except EMPNO and DEPTNO. Only three columns are printed in the second loop, you can try all columns.

Example 2

```
DECLARE
    TYPE emp_ty IS TABLE OF emp%ROWTYPE
        INDEX BY BINARY_INTEGER;

    emp_tb    emp_ty;
BEGIN
    FOR i IN 1 .. 10
    LOOP
        emp_tb (i).empno         := i;
        emp_tb (i).ename         := 'USMAN';
        emp_tb (i).job           := 'CLERK';
        emp_tb (i).mgr           := 4522;
        emp_tb (i).hiredate      := SYSDATE;
        emp_tb (i).sal           := 10000;
        emp_tb (i).comm          := .5;
        emp_tb (i).deptno        := i;
        emp_tb (i).age           := 25;
    END LOOP;

    FOR i IN 1 .. 10
    LOOP
        DBMS_OUTPUT.put_line (    emp_tb (i).empno
                             ||  ' '
                             ||  emp_tb (i).ename
                             ||  ' '
                             ||  emp_tb (i).job
                             );
    END LOOP;
END;
/
Output
1 USMAN CLERK
2 USMAN CLERK
3 USMAN CLERK
4 USMAN CLERK
5 USMAN CLERK
6 USMAN CLERK
7 USMAN CLERK
8 USMAN CLERK
PL/SQL procedure successfully completed.
```

3. Nested Tables

Syntax

TYPE type_name IS TABLE OF datatype [NOT NULL]
Table_name type_name;

Nested tables are very similar to associative arrays except that they are not indexed so INDEX BY clause is not used. Nested tables must be initialized before use and must be extended to created a new record by using method EXTEND before assigning values to a new record because they are not indexed. The following example is very similar to the above one except that INTEXT BY clause is not being used so to initialize the table EMP_TY( ) is used because a nested table must be initialized before use, EXTEND method is used to created a new row before assigning a value and inside EMP_TB nested table LAST method is used to refer latest created row.

Nested tables and Varrays are particularly useful when the table type is created in the database which is covered in coming lessons.

Example 1

```
DECLARE
    TYPE emp_ty IS TABLE OF emp%ROWTYPE;

    emp_tb    emp_ty := emp_ty ();
BEGIN
    FOR i IN 1 .. 10
    LOOP
        emp_tb.EXTEND;
        emp_tb (emp_tb.LAST).empno       := i;
        emp_tb (emp_tb.LAST).ename       := 'USMAN';
        emp_tb (emp_tb.LAST).job         := 'CLERK';
        emp_tb (emp_tb.LAST).mgr         := 4522;
        emp_tb (emp_tb.LAST).hiredate    := SYSDATE;
        emp_tb (emp_tb.LAST).sal         := 10000;
        emp_tb (emp_tb.LAST).comm        := .5;
        emp_tb (emp_tb.LAST).deptno      := i;
        emp_tb (emp_tb.LAST).age         := 25;
    END LOOP;

    FOR i IN 1 .. 10
    LOOP
        DBMS_OUTPUT.put_line (    emp_tb (i).empno
                             ||  ' '
                             ||  emp_tb (i).ename
                             ||  ' '
                             ||  emp_tb (i).job
                             );
    END LOOP;
END;
/
Output
1 USMAN CLERK
2 USMAN CLERK
3 USMAN CLERK
4 USMAN CLERK
5 USMAN CLERK
6 USMAN CLERK
7 USMAN CLERK
8 USMAN CLERK
9 USMAN CLERK
10 USMAN CLERK
PL/SQL procedure successfully completed.
```

4. Varrays

Varrays are similar to Nested tables, only the difference is that in varray the number of the elements is fixed in advance.

Syntax

TYPE type_name IS VARRAY(varray size) OF DATATYPE||RECORD TYPE;
Varray_var type_name;

TYPE indicates that a type is going to generate, type_name is any suitable name for the type, IS VARRAY indicates that it is VARRAY that is going to generate, OF DATA TYPE is the data type of the elements of varray,RECORD TYPE indicates that a varray can hold more then one column.

The following example uses varray, Note that varray is similarly used as nested tables inspite that its elements are fixed, This array can only hold 3 elements as VARRAY(3) is fixed.

Example 1

```
--use of varray
DECLARE
    TYPE v_ty IS VARRAY (3) OF VARCHAR2 (30);

    v_tb   v_ty := v_ty ('farhan', 'ali', 'arain');
BEGIN
    FOR i IN v_tb.FIRST .. v_tb.LAST
    LOOP
       DBMS_OUTPUT.put_line (v_tb (i));
    END LOOP;
END;
/
Output
farhan
ali
arain
PL/SQL procedure successfully completed.
```
**Note: that nested tables and varrays can also be declared at database level that is quite confusing; we will cover database types in coming chapter name 'Oracle object type'.
There is not any visible difference in nested tables and varrays inspite that varrays element's numbers are fixed at declaration time.**

5. Collection Methods

EXTEND
EXTEND is used to increase the size of a collection.

FIRST and LAST
FIRST refers to the first record of a table and LAST refers to the last record of the table

EXISTS
Returns TRUE if the element exists in the table, if you refer to a nonexistent element the error SUBSCRIPT_OUTSIDE_LIMIT comes, you can avoid the error by using this method.

COUNT
COUNT returns the number of rows in a table

PRIOR and NEXT
PRIOR returns the previous row of the row specified in the method argument, PRIOR (5) will return 4th element, NEXT returns the next row specified in the method argument.

TRIM
TRIM removes last element from the table, TRIM(n) removes n element from the end of the table.

Note: that EXTEND and TRIM methods are not allowed in Associative Arrays.

New enhancements in Oracle database 10G

One of the enhancements is that one collection can be assigned to other by using insert, update and delete statements or a subprogram call.
You can use operator such as SET, MULTISET UNION, MULTISET INTERSECT, and MULTISET EXCEPT to transform nested tables as part of an assignment statement.
To assign one collection to other collection both the collections should base on same collection type. The following example creates two type l_type and l_type2 and three collections.Collections v_grp1 and v_grp2 are based on same type l_type so they can be directly assigned to each other.

```
Exampel 1

DECLARE
    TYPE l_type IS TABLE OF VARCHAR2 (20);

    TYPE l_type2 IS TABLE OF VARCHAR2 (20);

    v_grp1    l_type  := l_type ('FARHAN', 'ALI', 'ARAIN');
    v_grp2    l_type  := l_type ('A', 'B', 'C');
    v_grp3    l_type2 := l_type2 ('F');
BEGIN
    --will work, both collections are based on type l_type
    v_grp2    := v_grp1;

    --will not work because they are based on different types
    --v_grp3:=v_grp1;
    FOR i IN v_grp2.FIRST .. v_grp2.LAST
    LOOP
        DBMS_OUTPUT.put_line (v_grp2 (i));
    END LOOP;
END;
/
Output
FARHAN
ALI
ARAIN
PL/SQL procedure successfully completed.
```

6. Collection Operators

MULTISET UNION
        It is equal to UNION ALL operator of SQL, it selects all the values of two collections and returns.

MULTISET UNION DISTINCT
        It is equal to UNION operator of SQL, it selects all the values of two collections escapes common values with one value an returns.

MULTISET INTERSECT
        It is equal to INERSECT operator of SQL, it selects all common values of two collections and returns.

MULTISET INTERSECT DISTINCT
        It is equal to INERSECT operator of SQL, it selects all common values of two collections escapes common values with one value and returns.

MULTISET EXCEPT
        It is equal to the MINUS operator of SQL, it selects first collection's values does minus the second collection's values and returns.

MULTISET EXCEPT DISTINCT
        It is equal to the MINUS operator of SQL, it selects first collection's values does minus the second collection's values and escapes common values with one value and returns.

Following example uses MULTISET UNION that is equal to UNION ALL operator which is use with SELECT statements.
Three collections l_col_1, l_col_2 and l_col_3 are declared based on one base type t_colors, two collection l_col_1 and l_col_2 are initialized. In the executable section MULTISET UNION is used with the l_col_1 and l_col_2 and the are assigned to l_col_3 until which has no value, the new values of l_col_3 are printed by using the loop.

Example 1

```
DECLARE
            TYPE t_colors IS TABLE OF VARCHAR2(10);
             l_col_1 t_colors := t_colors('Red', 'Green', 'Blue');
             l_col_2 t_colors := t_colors('Yellow', 'Orange','Blue');
             l_col_3 t_colors;
BEGIN
            -- Expression assignments.
            l_col_3 := l_col_1 MULTISET UNION l_col_2;
            for i in l_col_3.first..l_col_3.last loop
            dbms_output.put_line(l_col_3(i));
            end loop;
END;
/
Output
Red
Green
Blue
Yellow
Orange
Blue
PL/SQL procedure successfully completed.
```

You can use DISTINCT keyword with MULTISET UNION to get the funcrionality of UNION. The following example used DISTINCT keyword , In the out put Blue comes only once.

Example

```
DECLARE
            TYPE t_colors IS TABLE OF VARCHAR2(10);
             l_col_1 t_colors := t_colors('Red', 'Green', 'Blue');
             l_col_2 t_colors := t_colors('Yellow', 'Orange','Blue');
             l_col_3 t_colors;
BEGIN
            -- Expression assignments.
            l_col_3 := l_col_1 MULTISET UNION DISTINCT l_col_2;
            for i in l_col_3.first..l_col_3.last loop
            dbms_output.put_line(l_col_3(i));
            end loop;
END;
/
Output
Red
Green
Blue
Yellow
Orange PL/SQL procedure successfully completed.
```

Following example covers all collection operators in detail, because a loop is used to print the contents of a collection so a procedure is created for this functionality.

Example 2

```
DECLARE
          TYPE t_colors IS TABLE OF VARCHAR2(10);
          l_col_1 t_colors := t_colors('Red', 'Green', 'Blue', 'Green',
'Blue');
          l_col_2 t_colors := t_colors('Red', 'Green', 'Yellow', 'Green');
          l_col_3 t_colors;
      PROCEDURE display (p_text  IN  VARCHAR2,
                   p_col   IN  t_colors) IS
      BEGIN
              DBMS_OUTPUT.put_line(CHR(10) || p_text);
              FOR i IN p_col.first .. p_col.last LOOP
              DBMS_OUTPUT.put_line(p_col(i));
      END LOOP;
      END;
BEGIN
          -- Basic assignment.
          l_col_3 := l_col_1;
          display('Direct Assignment:', l_col_3);
          -- Expression assignments.
          l_col_3 := l_col_1 MULTISET UNION l_col_2;
          display('MULTISET UNION:', l_col_3);
          l_col_3 := l_col_1 MULTISET UNION DISTINCT l_col_2;
          display('MULTISET UNION DISTINCT:', l_col_3);
          l_col_3 := l_col_1 MULTISET INTERSECT l_col_2;
          display('MULTISET INTERSECT:', l_col_3);
          l_col_3 := l_col_1 MULTISET INTERSECT DISTINCT l_col_2;
          display('MULTISET INTERSECT DISTINCT:', l_col_3);
          l_col_3 := l_col_1 MULTISET EXCEPT l_col_2;
          display('MULTISET EXCEPT:', l_col_3);
          l_col_3 := l_col_1 MULTISET EXCEPT DISTINCT l_col_2;
          display('MULTISET EXCEPT DISTINCT:', l_col_3);
          END;
/
```
Output
Direct Assignment:
Red
Green
Blue
Green
Blue
MULTISET UNION:

Red
Green
Blue
Green
Blue
Red

Green
Yellow
Green
MULTISET UNION DISTINCT:
Red
Green
Blue
Yellow
MULTISET INTERSECT:
Red
Green
Green
MULTISET INTERSECT DISTINCT:
Red
Green
MULTISET EXCEPT:
Blue
Blue
MULTISET EXCEPT DISTINCT:
Blue
PL/SQL procedure successfully completed.

Summary

In this chapter you have learned that the PLSQL collections are just like tables but collections can only store data temporarily, Associative array are used to store data temporarily for perforating complex calculations, associative arrays can have one or more columns and always have one column which contains the sequencial number as index, Nested tables are similar to that of associative arrays but nested tables do not contain index and nested tables are initialized before usage, VARRAYs can contain the number of elements specified by the user in the declaration.

Exercise

1. Create an array that store all the days of the current month in the format 'MONDAY 1st JUN' and print them in the similar format.

2. Create a two dimension associative array, a nested table and a varray as of the above example, the only difference should be that these will have two columns, First column should store the counter and second should store days of current month. Print them in this format '1 MONDAY'.

9 CURSORS

In this chapter you will learn about

Introduction to cursors
Implicit cursors
Explicit cursors
Open, fetch and close statements
Cursor for loop
Where current of cursor
Cursor variable

Introduction to cursors

Whenever any SQL statement is executed an area in memory is reserved where the statement is parsed and executed that area in memory is called a cursor.
There are two types of cursors in PL/SQL

1. Implicit cursors

These cursors are created and managed by the oracle whenever any DML statement is executed or whenever select statement is executed.

2. Explicit cursors

Explicit cursors are defined by the user to individually process multiple rows returned by a select statement.

In this chapter explicit cursors are discussed.

Declaring an explicit cursor

Syntax

CURSOR cursor_name[parameters]
IS
  Query
[FOR UPDATE[OF(columns)][NOWAIT]];

CURSOR keyword defines that it is the cursor which is going to generate, cursor_name specifies the cursor name, [parameters] define the parameters which are used inside the query of cursor, Query defines the select statement that will return more than one rows, FOR UPDATE specifies that the rows are not updated by other users when cursor is open, it can be specified for some specific columns as well. [NOWAIT] ensures that if the rows are locked by other users and a lock cannot be achieved then exit the program on execution.

Opening, fetching, processing and closing the cursor

After declaring cursor you have to follow some steps to work with cursor, these include
Open the cursor, fetch the records, do the processing and close the cursor.

Opening the cursor

Cursor is opened before working with it, cursor is opened by using the following syntax

OPEN cursor_name;

FETCHING the records

FETCH statement is used to get one row from the cursor at a time so the FETCH statement is always used within the LOOP, following syntax is used to FETCH the records.

FETCH cursor_name INTO [variables][user defined record]

The variables after INTO takes the value of the columns of the cursor's SELECT statement, A user defined record can also be used here.

Doing processing

After fetching a record its values are available in variables so any processing can be done on the values.

CLOSE the cursor

A cursor needs to be closed after working on it; it will consume the memory otherwise, Cursor is closed by using the following syntax

CLOSE cursor_name;

Cursor attributes

Cursor attributes are used to take the status of the cursor; there are the following cursor attributes

Cursor%FOUND　　　Returns TRUE when the cursor's FETCH statement fetches a Record, FALSE when the record is not fetched and NULL before FETCH statement.

Cursor%NOTFOUND　Returns FALSE when the cursor's FETCH statement fetches a Record, TRUE when the record is not fetched and NULL before FETCH statement.

Cursor%ROWCOUNT Returns the number of row returned by the FETCH statement.

Cursor%ISOPEN　　　Returns TRUE when the cursor is open and FALSE otherwise.

Following example uses cursor, Cursor declared in the declaration section contain a select statement which selects three columns EMPNO, ENAME and SAL from EMP table. Three variables are declared to get the values of the cursor.
In the Executable section cursor is opened, Inside loop the FETCH statement is used to fetch the cursor into variables, Cursor attribute %NOTFOUND is used to exit the loop when there are no more rows and cursor is close at the end by using CLOSE statement.

This is the simplest example that shows the use of SELECT statement returning multiple rows inside a PLSQL block.

Example 1

```
DECLARE
   CURSOR emp_cur
   IS
      SELECT empno,
             ename,
             sal
      FROM   emp;

   l_empno    emp.empno%TYPE;
   l_ename    emp.ename%TYPE;
   l_sal      emp.sal%TYPE;
BEGIN
   OPEN emp_cur;

   LOOP
      FETCH emp_cur
      INTO  l_empno,
            l_ename,
            l_sal;

      EXIT WHEN emp_cur%NOTFOUND;
      DBMS_OUTPUT.put_line (l_empno || ' ' || l_ename || ' ' || l_sal);
   END LOOP;
END;
/

Output
1122 FARHAN 15000
9866 CHANGED 8000
7566 Irfan 8000
7654 MARTIN 8000
7698 BLAKE 8000
7782 SHAHZAD 8000
7788 SCOTT 8000
7839 KINGS 8000
7844 TURNER 8000
7876 ADAMS 8000
7900 JAMES 8000
7902 FORD 8000
9898 TEST 8000
PL/SQL procedure successfully completed.
```

Same block can be written by using a while loop, In this example WHILE loop only executes if the FETCH statement fetches a record that's why FETCH statement is also written before loop otherwise the %FOUND returns null during first iteration and loop will not execute even once.

EXAMPLE 2

```
DECLARE
    CURSOR emp_cur
    IS
        SELECT empno,
               ename,
               sal
        FROM   emp;

    l_empno    emp.empno%TYPE;
    l_ename    emp.ename%TYPE;
    l_sal      emp.sal%TYPE;
BEGIN
    OPEN emp_cur;

    FETCH emp_cur
    INTO  l_empno,
          l_ename,
          l_sal;

    WHILE emp_cur%FOUND
    LOOP
        DBMS_OUTPUT.put_line (l_empno || ' ' || l_ename || ' ' || l_sal);

        FETCH emp_cur
        INTO  l_empno,
              l_ename,
              l_sal;

    END LOOP;
END;
/
Output
1122 FARHAN 15000
9866 CHANGED 8000
7566 Irfan 8000
7654 MARTIN 8000
7698 BLAKE 8000
7782 SHAHZAD 8000
7788 SCOTT 8000
7839 KINGS 8000
7844 TURNER 8000
7876 ADAMS 8000
7900 JAMES 8000
7902 FORD 8000
9898 TEST 8000
PL/SQL procedure successfully completed.
```

You can also use FOR loop but in FOR loop you have to specify the number of iterations the loop will execute so it is difficult to specify that how many rows the cursor will return, Use of FOR loop is as following.

Example 3

```
DECLARE
   CURSOR emp_cur
   IS
      SELECT *
      FROM    emp;

   v_rec    emp%ROWTYPE;
BEGIN
   OPEN emp_cur;

   FOR i IN 1 .. 5
   LOOP
      FETCH emp_cur
      INTO  v_rec;

      DBMS_OUTPUT.put_line (v_rec.empno || ' ' || v_rec.sal);
   END LOOP;
END;
/
```

When a cursor is fetched without opening it give the error 'INVALID CURSOR' as following

```
DECLARE
    CURSOR emp_cur
    IS
        SELECT empno,
               ename,
               sal
        FROM   emp;

    l_empno    emp.empno%TYPE;
    l_ename    emp.ename%TYPE;
    l_sal      emp.sal%TYPE;
BEGIN
    LOOP
        FETCH emp_cur
        INTO  l_empno,
              l_ename,
              l_sal;

        EXIT WHEN emp_cur%NOTFOUND;
        DBMS_OUTPUT.put_line (l_empno || ' ' || l_ename || ' ' || l_sal);
    END LOOP;
END;
/
```
Output
DECLARE
*

ERROR at line 1:
ORA-01001: invalid cursor
ORA-06512: at line 13

Cursor%ISOPEN can be used to check that weather the cursor is open or not, the following example checks the cursor and opens it if the cursor is closed.

```
--Use of cursor%ISOPEN attribute
DECLARE
    CURSOR emp_cur
    IS
        SELECT empno,
               ename,
               sal
        FROM   emp;

    l_empno    emp.empno%TYPE;
    l_ename    emp.ename%TYPE;
    l_sal      emp.sal%TYPE;
BEGIN
    IF NOT emp_cur%ISOPEN
    THEN
        OPEN emp_cur;
    END IF;

    LOOP
        FETCH emp_cur
        INTO  l_empno,
              l_ename,
              l_sal;

        EXIT WHEN emp_cur%NOTFOUND;
        DBMS_OUTPUT.put_line (l_empno || ' ' || l_ename || ' ' || l_sal);
    END LOOP;
END;
/

Output
1122 FARHAN 15000
9866 CHANGED 8000
7566 Irfan 8000
7654 MARTIN 8000
7698 BLAKE 8000
7782 SHAHZAD 8000
7788 SCOTT 8000
7839 KINGS 8000
7844 TURNER 8000
7876 ADAMS 8000
7900 JAMES 8000
7902 FORD 8000
9898 TEST 8000
PL/SQL procedure successfully completed.
```

Parameters in cursors

Parameters can be used inside a cursor as in the following example.
In the following example a parameter of type number is passed and used in the where clause, the cursor returns the number of rows only satisfying the where clause. In the OPEN statement the parameters value 1122 is given so the cursor is returning only one row.

```
Example 1

DECLARE
    CURSOR emp_cur (p_empno NUMBER)
    IS
        SELECT empno,
               ename,
               sal
        FROM   emp
        WHERE  empno = p_empno;

    l_empno    emp.empno%TYPE;
    l_ename    emp.ename%TYPE;
    l_sal      emp.sal%TYPE;
BEGIN
    OPEN emp_cur (7900);

    LOOP
        FETCH emp_cur
        INTO  l_empno,
              l_ename,
              l_sal;

        EXIT WHEN emp_cur%NOTFOUND;
        DBMS_OUTPUT.put_line (l_empno || ' ' || l_ename || ' ' || l_sal);
    END LOOP;
END;
/

Output
7900 JAMES 8000
PL/SQL procedure successfully completed.
```

Note: Length is not needed while the data type of parameter is specified.

The following example is used to explain the use of parameters in detail, two cursors are used in the example, the outer cursor selects department's information and the inner cursor selects the employee's information that are of the specific department of the outer cursor.
The department number is passed as parameter to the cursor cur_emp.

Note: the use of ROWTYPE records instead of variables to get the values in the FETCH statements.

Example 2

```
DECLARE
   CURSOR cur_dept
   IS
      SELECT *
      FROM   dept;

   CURSOR cur_emp (p_deptno emp.deptno%TYPE)
   IS
      SELECT *
      FROM   emp
      WHERE  deptno = p_deptno;

   rec_dept    dept%ROWTYPE;
   rec_emp     emp%ROWTYPE;
BEGIN
   OPEN cur_dept;

   LOOP
      FETCH cur_dept
      INTO  rec_dept;

      EXIT WHEN cur_dept%NOTFOUND;
      DBMS_OUTPUT.put_line (   'DEPARTMENT IS '
                            || rec_dept.deptno
                            || ' '
                            || rec_dept.dname
                           );
      DBMS_OUTPUT.put_line ('.......EMPLOYEES ARE........');

      OPEN cur_emp (rec_dept.deptno);

      LOOP
         FETCH cur_emp
         INTO  rec_emp;

         EXIT WHEN cur_emp%NOTFOUND;
         DBMS_OUTPUT.put_line (   'EMPNO '



                            || rec_emp.empno
                            || ' ENAME '
                            || rec_emp.ename
```

```
                              );
     END LOOP;

     CLOSE cur_emp;
   END LOOP;

   CLOSE cur_dept;
END;
/
```

```
Output
DEPARTMENT IS 20 FINANC
.......EMPLOYEES ARE........
EMPNO 9866 ENAME CHANGED
EMPNO 7566 ENAME Irfan
EMPNO 7788 ENAME SCOTT
EMPNO 7876 ENAME ADAMS
EMPNO 7902 ENAME FORD
DEPARTMENT IS 30 IMB
.......EMPLOYEES ARE........
EMPNO 1122 ENAME FARHAN
EMPNO 7654 ENAME MARTIN
EMPNO 7698 ENAME BLAKE
EMPNO 7844 ENAME TURNER
EMPNO 7900 ENAME JAMES
DEPARTMENT IS 40 LOGISTICS123
.......EMPLOYEES ARE........
EMPNO 9898 ENAME TEST
DEPARTMENT IS 10 ALARA
.......EMPLOYEES ARE........
EMPNO 7782 ENAME SHAHZAD
EMPNO 7839 ENAME KINGS

PL/SQL procedure successfully completed.
```

CURSOR FOR loop

CURSOR FOR loop is used to avoid several steps like opening the cursor, fetching the cursor and closing the cursor.
CURSOR FOR loop automatically opens the cursor, fetches the cursor and closes the cursor.
The following example uses the CURSOR FOR loop, note that OPEN, FETCH and CLOSE statements are not used.

Example 1

```
DECLARE
   CURSOR emp_cur
   IS
      SELECT empno,
             ename,
             sal
      FROM    emp;

   TYPE emp_rec_ty IS RECORD (
      l_empno   NUMBER,
      l_ename   VARCHAR2 (15),
      l_sal     NUMBER
   );

   emp_rec    emp_rec_ty;
BEGIN
   FOR emp_rec IN emp_cur
   LOOP
      DBMS_OUTPUT.put_line (    emp_rec.empno
                           || ' '
                           || emp_rec.ename
                           || ' '
                           || emp_rec.sal
                           );
   END LOOP;
END;
/

Output
1122 FARHAN 15000
9866 CHANGED 8000
7566 Irfan 8000
7654 MARTIN 8000
7876 ADAMS 8000
7900 JAMES 8000
7902 FORD 8000
9898 TEST 8000
PL/SQL procedure successfully completed.
```

The following example uses the parameter with CURSOR FOR loop

Example 2

```
DECLARE
    CURSOR emp_cur (p_ename VARCHAR2)
    IS
        SELECT empno,
               ename,
               sal
        FROM    emp
        WHERE   ename LIKE '%' || p_ename || '%';

    TYPE emp_rec_ty IS RECORD (
        l_empno   NUMBER,
        l_ename   VARCHAR2 (15),
        l_sal     NUMBER
    );

    emp_rec   emp_rec_ty;
BEGIN
    FOR emp_rec IN emp_cur ('MARTIN')
    LOOP
        DBMS_OUTPUT.put_line (   emp_rec.empno
                              || ' '
                              || emp_rec.ename
                              || ' '
                              || emp_rec.sal
                              );
    END LOOP;
END;
/

Output
7654 MARTIN 8000
PL/SQL procedure successfully completed.
```

CURSOR FOR loop with SELECT statement

SELECT statement can be used with CURSOR FOR loop in this case cursor needs not to declare in the Declaration section as explained in the following example. Cursor attributes cannot be used with CURSOR FOR loop having select statement.

Example 1

```
DECLARE
   TYPE emp_rec_ty IS RECORD (
      l_empno    NUMBER,
      l_ename    VARCHAR2 (15),
      l_sal      NUMBER
   );

   emp_rec    emp_rec_ty;
BEGIN
   FOR emp_rec IN (SELECT empno,
                          ename,
                          sal
                   FROM    emp)
   LOOP
      DBMS_OUTPUT.put_line (   emp_rec.empno
                            || ' '
                            || emp_rec.ename
                            || ' '
                            || emp_rec.sal
                           );
   END LOOP;
END;
/
```

The following example shows the use of parameter with CURSOR FOR LOOP having SELECT statement in the loop;

Example 2

```
DECLARE
    TYPE emp_rec_ty IS RECORD (
        l_empno     NUMBER,
        l_ename     VARCHAR2 (15),
        l_sal       NUMBER
    );

    emp_rec     emp_rec_ty;
    v_empno     NUMBER          := 7900;
BEGIN
    FOR emp_rec IN (SELECT empno,
                           ename,
                           sal
                    FROM    emp
                    WHERE   empno = v_empno)
    LOOP
        DBMS_OUTPUT.put_line (    emp_rec.empno
                              || ' '
                              || emp_rec.ename
                              || ' '
                              || emp_rec.sal
                             );
    END LOOP;
END;
/
Output
7900 JAMES 950
PL/SQL procedure successfully completed.
```

WHERE CURRENT OF cursor

Where current of cursor is used in UPDATE or DELETE statements to refer the current row of the cursor.

Whenever WHERE CURRENT OF CURSOR is used the cursor must be declared by using the FOR UPDATE clause.

The following example uses WHERE CURRENT OF CURSOR in the update statement and row in the EMP table is referred without writing any condition in the WHERE clause.

```
Example 1

DECLARE
    CURSOR emp_cursor
    IS
        SELECT          *
        FROM            emp
        WHERE           empno = 7900
        FOR UPDATE OF sal;
BEGIN
    FOR emp_record IN emp_cursor
    LOOP
        UPDATE emp
        SET sal = 1000
        WHERE CURRENT OF emp_cursor;
    END LOOP;

    COMMIT;
END;
/
Output
PLSQL procedure successfully completed
```

If any particular record is going to update by using WHERE CURRENT OF CURSOR and that record is updated by another user then the execution of the program will halt until the changes are committed or roll backed by the user who have done the changes, to avoid this NOWAIT keyword is used with WHERE CURRENT OF CURSOR which will terminate the program if the particular record has been locked by other user as following

```
DECLARE
    CURSOR emp_cursor
    IS
        SELECT          *
        FROM            emp
        WHERE           empno = 7900
        FOR UPDATE OF sal NOWAIT;
BEGIN
```

```
FOR emp_record IN emp_cursor
    LOOP
        UPDATE emp
        SET sal = 1000
        WHERE CURRENT OF emp_cursor;
    END LOOP;

    COMMIT;
END;
/
```
Output
PLSQL procedure successfully completed

Cursor Variable

CURSOR VARIABLES are dynamic alternative of static cursors; CURSOR VARIALBES are opened at run time and can change queries at run time hence CURSOR VARIALBE are used to write dynamic select statements that return multiple rows.
CURSOR VARIABLES can also pass set of data to and from program units.
CURSOR VARIABLES are covered in coming chapter 'Dynamic SQL' in greater detail.

The following example shows simple use of CURSOR VARIABLE.
The example creates a type emp_cur_type of type REF CURSOR which specifies emp%ROWTYPE as return type, cursor variable emp_cur is defined of type emp_cur_ty.
Cursor variable emp_cur is opened with select statement specified.
All other steps are similar as that of static cursor.

Example 1

```
DECLARE
    TYPE emp_cur_ty IS REF CURSOR
        RETURN emp%ROWTYPE;

    emp_cur     emp_cur_ty;
    l_emp       emp%ROWTYPE;
BEGIN
    OPEN emp_cur FOR
        SELECT *
        FROM    emp;

    LOOP
        FETCH emp_cur
        INTO   l_emp;


    EXIT WHEN emp_cur%NOTFOUND;
        DBMS_OUTPUT.put_line (l_emp.empno || ' ' || l_emp.ename);
```

```
    END LOOP;

    CLOSE emp_cur;
END;
/
```
Output
1122 FARHAN
9866 CHANGED
7566 Irfan
7654 MARTIN
7698 BLAKE
7782 SHAHZAD
7788 SCOTT
7839 KINGS
7844 TURNER
7876 ADAMS
7900 JAMES
7902 FORD
9898 TEST
PL/SQL procedure successfully completed.

Summary

In this chapter you have learned that whenever any SQL statement is executed an area in memory is reserved where the statement is parsed and executed that area in memory is called a CURSOR. There are two types of CURSORS in PL/SQL EXPLICIT CURSORS and IMPLICIT CURSORS, IMPLICIT CURSORS are managed by oracle, explicit cursors are used to individually process multiple rows returned by a query, a cursor must be opened before fetch and cursor must be closed at the end. A CURSOR FOR LOOP opens the cursor, fetches the cursor and closes the cursor automatically. WHERE CURRENT OF CURSOR is used to update the current row of the cursor, Whenever WHERE CURRENT OF CURSOR is used cursor must be defined with FOR UPDATE clause so that any other user can not update the record.
CURSOR VARIABLES are dynamic alternative of static cursors; CURSOR VARIALBES are opened at run time and can change queries at run time hence CURSOR VARIALBE are used to write dynamic select statements that return multiple rows.

Exercise

    1. What is wrong with the following statement

```
DECLARE
   CURSOR emp_cur
   IS
      SELECT empno,
             ename,
             sal
      FROM   emp;

   l_empno    emp.empno%TYPE;
   l_ename    emp.ename%TYPE;
   l_sal      emp.sal%TYPE;
BEGIN

   FETCH emp_cur
   INTO  l_empno,
         l_ename,
         l_sal;

   WHILE emp_cur%FOUND
   LOOP
      DBMS_OUTPUT.put_line (l_empno || ' ' || l_ename || ' ' || l_sal);

      FETCH emp_cur
      INTO  l_empno,
            l_ename,
            l_sal;

   END LOOP;
END;
/
```

    2. Execute the following statements to create a table and insert some rows, Write a program that should use a cursor, the cursor should accept parameters(username, password) and select the data accordingly, if the row is found against username and password then show the message 'Provide access' .

```
CREATE TABLE users(user_name VARCHAR2(50),PASSWORD VARCHAR2(25))
/
INSERT INTO users
VALUES      ('FARHAN',
             'FAR1234*'
             )
/
```

```
INSERT INTO users
VALUES      ('ALI',
             '1234AL'
            )
/
INSERT INTO users
VALUES      ('HINA',
             'HINAH'
            )
/
COMMIT
/
```

3. Do the above task by using cursor for loop.

4. Write a program that should update DNAME column of dept table for any particular department by using WHERE CURRENT OF CURSOR.

10 EXCEPTION HANDLING

In this chapter you will learn about

What is an exception?
Pre defined exceptions
User defined exceptions
Undefined exceptions
RAISE_APPLICATION_ERROR procedure

What is an exception?

Exception is the error that can cause a program to terminate abnormally. For example if a SELECT Statement in the Executable section returns no rows, an exception comes and terminates the program unconditionally.

The following example raises an exception because select statement returns no rows as no record is found for EMPNO 8567.

Example 1

```
--Returning Employee name
DECLARE
    v_name    VARCHAR2 (50);
BEGIN
    SELECT ename
    INTO   v_name
    FROM   emp e
    WHERE  e.empno = 8567;

    DBMS_OUTPUT.put_line (v_name);
END;
/
```

Output
DECLARE
*

ERROR at line 1:
ORA-01403: no data found
ORA-06512: at line 4

This exception can be trapped (handled), if user wants to ignore this exception or want to perform his own defined actions as following

```
DECLARE
    v_name    VARCHAR2 (50);
BEGIN
    SELECT ename
    INTO   v_name
    FROM   emp e
    WHERE  e.empno = '8567';

    DBMS_OUTPUT.put_line (v_name);
EXCEPTION
    WHEN NO_DATA_FOUND
    THEN
       DBMS_OUTPUT.put_line ('No employee exists with this number');
END;
/

Output
```
No employee exists with this number

Exception types

There are three types of exceptions
Pre defined
Undefined
User defined

Predefined

Syntax

```
BEGIN
   STATEMENT 1
   STATEMENT 2
   ..................
EXCEPTION WHEN CODITON THEN
   STATEMENT 1
   STATEMENT 2
END;
```

These types of exceptions are defined by oracle, for example if SELECT Statement in executable section returns now rows then exception NO_DATA_FOUND is raised or when SELECT Statement returns more than one rows then exception TOO_MANY_ROWS is raised. This type of Exceptions can be trapped by simply referring them in the exception section as shown in the following example

Example 1

```
--More than one row is returned by select statement and hence exception is raised
DECLARE
    v_name    VARCHAR2 (50);
BEGIN
    SELECT ename
    INTO   v_name
    FROM   emp e;

    DBMS_OUTPUT.put_line (v_name);
END;
/

Output
DECLARE
*
ERROR at line 1:
ORA-01422: exact fetch returns more than requested number of rows
ORA-06512: at line 4
```

This error can simply be trapped as following

```
DECLARE
   v_name    VARCHAR2 (50);
BEGIN
   SELECT ename
   INTO   v_name
   FROM   emp e;

   DBMS_OUTPUT.put_line (v_name);
EXCEPTION
   WHEN TOO_MANY_ROWS
   THEN
      DBMS_OUTPUT.put_line ('More than expected number of rows returned');
END;
/

Output
More than expected number of rows returned
```

Undefined Exceptions

All the Exceptions are not defined in oracle so these exception needs to be associated with proper error name.
For that purpose an exception is defined in the declaration section and is associated with the error code number by using compiler directive PRAGMA EXCEPTON_INIT.
PRAGMA EXCEPTION_INIT takes two parameters; First parameter is user defined exception name and second is error code.

In the following example there is a delete statement for department 20 but department cannot be deleted because Child record exists in the EMP table so the error -2292 is raised. This error number is associated with the user defined Exception V_EXP by using PARAGA EXECEPTION_INIT and handled in the exception section.

Example 1

```
DECLARE
   v_exp    EXCEPTION;
   PRAGMA EXCEPTION_INIT (v_exp, -2292);
BEGIN
   DELETE FROM dept
   WHERE        deptno = 20;
  DBMS_OUTPUT.put_line ('Dept deleted');
EXCEPTION
   WHEN v_exp
   THEN
      DBMS_OUTPUT.put_line ('Can not delete record when a Child record is
found');
END;
/
```

```
Output
Cannot delete record, when a Child record is found

PL/SQL procedure successfully completed.
```

User defined exception

Syntax

```
DECLARE
 V_exeception EXCEPTION;
BEGIN
 STATEMENT 1;
 RAISE V_Exception;
 STATEMENT 2;
EXCEPTION
WHEN V_Exception THEN
 STATEMENT 1;
 STATEMENT 2;
END;
```

User defined EXCEPTION is the exception which is defined by the user, raised by the user and trapped by the user, this exception is used to terminate the program if user wants it on any specific condition. A user declares it in the DECLARATION section, then RAISES it for some specific condition in the executable section or in the exception section and handles it in EXCEPTION section. In the following example an EXCEPTION v_exp is defined in the declaration section, at run time user provides the value to substitution variable, if value is greater than 10 then exception is raised and trapped in the Exception Section.

```
EXAMPLE 1

--User defined Exception
DECLARE
    v_number    NUMBER      := &p_value;
    v_exp       EXCEPTION;
BEGIN
    IF v_number > 10
    THEN
       RAISE v_exp;
    END IF;

    DBMS_OUTPUT.put_line ('Number is smaller than 10');
EXCEPTION
    WHEN v_exp
    THEN
       DBMS_OUTPUT.put_line ('Number is greater than 10'); END;
/
Output
Enter value for p_value: 15
old    2: v_number number:=&p_value;
new    2: v_number number:=15;
Number is greater than 10
PL/SQL procedure successfully completed.
```

The RAISE_APPLICATION_ERROR Procedure

The RAISE_APPLICATION_ERROR is a built in procedure which can be used as an alternative to user defined exceptions.
The RAISE_APPLICATION_ERROR takes three arguments error_code, error_message and an optional keep_errors.

Syntax

Raise_application_error(error_code,error_message,keep_errors);

Error_code can be any number between -20000 to -29999, Error_message is any suitable message and Keep_errors is a BOOLEAN variable (TRUE or FALSE).
Keep_errors save the errors to an error stack when set to TRUE.
Keep_errors by default is FALSE which mean that RAISE_APPLICATION_ERROR does not save the error to the error stack.
The following example is similar as that of user defined exception; the user defined exception's functionality is achieved by only one line.
Raise_application_error shows the error in proper oracle style.

Example 1

```
--Use of Raise_application_error
DECLARE
   v_number    NUMBER := &p_value;
BEGIN
   IF v_number > 10
   THEN
      raise_application_error (-20001, 'Number is greater than 10');
   END IF;

   DBMS_OUTPUT.put_line ('Number is smaller than 10');
END;
/

Output
Enter value for p_value: 15
old    2:     v_number    NUMBER    := &p_value;
new    2:     v_number    NUMBER    := 15;
DECLARE
*
ERROR at line 1:
ORA-20001: Number is greater than 10
ORA-06512: at line 6
```

WHEN_OTHERS Exception handler

WHEN_OTHERS exception handler guarantees that no exception will be unhandled;
WHEN_OTHERS is used at the last in EXCEPTION section as shown in following example.

Example 1

```
--Use of WHEN-OTHERS clause
DECLARE
    v_name    VARCHAR2 (50);
    v_num     NUMBER (4);
BEGIN
    SELECT ename
    INTO   v_name
    FROM   emp e
    WHERE  empno = 7839;

    DBMS_OUTPUT.put_line (v_name);
    v_num     := 5867456;
EXCEPTION
    WHEN TOO_MANY_ROWS
    THEN
        DBMS_OUTPUT.put_line ('Query is returning more then one row');
    WHEN OTHERS
    THEN
        DBMS_OUTPUT.put_line (SQLERRM);
END;
/
Output
KINGS
ORA-06502: PL/SQL: numeric or value error: number precision too large
PL/SQL procedure successfully completed.
```

Note: that WHEN OTHERS is used at last in the EXCEPTION section so that any error other then the defined errors can be handled.

Summary

In this chapter you have learned that there are three types of exceptions Oracle Defined, Undefined and user defined.

Defined exception are handled by naming them in the exception section, Undefined exceptions are trapped by declaring an exception in the declaration section and associating it with error number by using PRAGMA exception_init compiler directive, User defined exceptions are used when user want to raise an exception on his own specific condition.

RAISE_APPLICATION_ERROR is an alternative of user defined exceptions and displays the error in slandered oracle style.

WHEN_OTHERS ensures that no exception is unhandled; it is used at last in exception section.

Exercise

1. Create a program to handle NO_DATA_FOUND exception.

2. Handle exception in the following example and give an appropriate message.

```
DECLARE
    v_name    VARCHAR2 (50);
BEGIN
    SELECT ename
    INTO   v_name
    FROM   emp e;
    DBMS_OUTPUT.put_line (v_name);
END;

--Handling TO_MANY_ROWS exception
DECLARE
    v_name    VARCHAR2 (50);
BEGIN
    SELECT ename
    INTO   v_name
    FROM   emp e;

    DBMS_OUTPUT.put_line (v_name);
EXCEPTION
    WHEN too_many_rows
    THEN
        DBMS_OUTPUT.put_line ('Query is returning more then one row');
END;
/
```

3. You want to delete the complete data of dept number 20 from dept and EMP table, while using the following query the undefined error rises because the child records are found how you can correct the query to delete the records of department 20 from dept and EMP table.

```
DECLARE
    v_exp    EXCEPTION;
    PRAGMA EXCEPTION_INIT (v_exp, -2292);
BEGIN
    DELETE FROM dept
    WHERE         deptno = 20;

    DELETE FROM emp
    WHERE         deptno = 20;

    DBMS_OUTPUT.put_line ('Dept deleted');
EXCEPTION
    WHEN v_exp
    THEN
        DBMS_OUTPUT.put_line
                    ('Can not delete the record, while the child records exist');
END;
```

4. Create a program that selects the salary of any employee and if the salary is greater than 5000 then raise a user defined exception, at last trap the exception and give a suitable message.

5. Create a program that selects the salary of any employee and if the salary is greater than 5000 then raise a user defined exception through RAIS_APPLICATION_ERROR.

6. What is wrong with the following program?

```
DECLARE
    v_name    VARCHAR2 (50);
    v_num     NUMBER (4);
BEGIN
    SELECT ename
    INTO    v_name
    FROM    emp e
    WHERE   empno = 7839;

    DBMS_OUTPUT.put_line (v_name);
    v_num     := 5867456;
EXCEPTION
    WHEN OTHERS
    THEN
        DBMS_OUTPUT.put_line (SQLERRM);

    WHEN TOO_MANY_ROWS
    THEN
        DBMS_OUTPUT.put_line ('Query is returning more than one row');
END;
/
```

11 INTRODUCTION TO SUBPROGRAMS

In this chapter you will learn about

What is a Subprogram?
What is difference between anonyms PL/SQL blocks and named PL/SQL blocks?
What are the benefits of subprograms?
How to call a subprogram

What is a Subprogram?

A subprogram is a named PL/SQL block that is used to perform some action (procedure) or compute a value to return (function). A subprogram is based on a standard block structure of PL/SQL block, the only difference is that PL/SQL blocks are written where they are required and program units are written by giving a specific name and are stored in database to call where they are required.
Once written, a program unit can be called from any place where their functionality is required, can be more than one place.

The following syntax differentiates between a PL/SQL block and a program unit.

Syntax for a program unit

<Header >IS|AS
--Variables, cursors or types
BEGIN
Statement 1;
Statement 2;
EXCEPTION
--Exception handling code
END;

Syntax of a PL/SQL Block

```
DECLARE
--Variables, cursors or types
BEGIN
Statement 1;
Statement 2;
EXCEPTION
--Exception handling code
END;
```

Note: that the only difference is that in PL/SQL block DECLARE keyword is used while in a program unit there is a <Header>.
A Header contains the type of the program unit, its name and its parameters, further explained in the coming lessons.

Benefits of Subprograms

Subprograms provide modularity, reusability, extensibility, maintainability, security, code clarity and improved performance.
PL/SQL code can be written in small subprograms (modules) and can be called where they are required instead of writing long anonyms PL/SQL block, the subprograms written can be reused in any place where their functionality is required thus improving reusability.
The program units can be extended by adding the code in the particular program unit without affecting other code or program units thus program units are easily extensible and maintainable.
Program units can be controlled for indirect access from non privileged user by assign security privileges and ensure that related actions are taken together or not at all by funneling activity for related tables through a single path thus improve security.
Program units improve security by avoiding reparsing for multiple users by exploiting shared SQL area, program units can be reparsed at compile time to avoid reparsing at runtime.
Program units improve code clarity by using appropriate identifier names and code formatting.

Invoking subprograms

Procedures and function can be invoked from a number of environments such as ISQL*plus, Oracle Forms Developer, Oracle Reports Developer, Oracle Discoverer, Oracle Portal and from other program units. Following examples shows how a previously created procedure "Login_secure" can be invoked from different environments.
Invoking from Oracle Forms developer or other program units as following

> Login_secure;

Invoking from ISQL* Plus

> Execute Login_secure;

Summary

In this lesson you have learned the difference between anonyms PL/SQL block and Named PL/SQL block (Program unit or subprogram) and how to invoke subprogram from different environments.

12 PROCEDURES

In this chapter you will learn about

What is a procedure?
What are the benefits of using procedure?
Create a procedure
Differentiate between format and actual parameters
What are parameter modes?
How to invoke procedures?
Exception handling in procedures
Difference between stand alone procedure and packaged procedure
Compile time warnings
Dropping a procedure

What is a Procedure?

A procedure is a named PL/SQL block (Subprogram) that is stored in the data base and can be invoked to perform some specific action. A procedure can accept parameters and be invoked; Procedure improves modularity, reusability, maintainability, extensibility and security.
For example In a form application it is required in several places (say 1000 places) that when some specific event occurs then the salary of an employee should increase by 10%, in forms you can directly write the code where there is a requirement as following

```
BEGIN
   UPDATE emp
   SET sal = sal + (sal * .10)
   WHERE  empno = :a;
END;
```

This code is needed wherever the functionality is required and in future if there is some change in the functionality then the code will be updated at all the places, while there is a simple solution to this just create a procedure with the above functionality and invoke it wherever the functionality is required.
If the functionality changes in future then change will be only in the one procedure as following

```
CREATE PROCEDURE increase_sal (p_empno NUMBER)
IS
BEGIN
   UPDATE emp
   SET sal = sal + (sal * .10)
   WHERE  empno = p_empno;
END;
```

You can call this procedure any where the functionality is required, even at 1000 places. By just referring the name as following

Increase_sal;

Creating a procedure

Syntax

```
CREATE [OR REPLACE] PROCEDURE name
[(parameter1 [MODE] datatype1,
Parameter2 [MODE] datatype1…..)]
IS|AS
BEGIN
Statement 1;
Statement 2;
EXCEPTION
--Exception Handling
END [name];
```

OR REPLACE option deletes the existing procedure and recreates it if the procedure already exists; the section between IS|AS and BEGIN is DECLARATION section though Declare keyword is not used in procedures, all other sections are similar to that of PL/SQL block.

Parameters and their MODE

Parameters are variables, parameters values are passed into or populated by the procedure depends upon MODE. MODE defines that either the parameter will pass the value into the procedure or it will populate from the procedure to take the value out of the procedure, MODE can be IN means value of the parameter is passed into the procedure, or MODE can be OUT means value is populated or returned from Procedure to outside, or MODE can be IN OUT means values is passed into the procedure and returned outside by the same parameter.

Data type defines the parameter data type that either it is of NUMBER, CHARACTER , DATE, data type's length cannot be defined in the parameters.
In the following example a procedure is created with name Increase_Sal, one parameter P_EMPNO of NUMBER data type is passed into procedure that is used in the where clause of the update statement.

When procedure is called from ISQL* Plus a value 7900 is passed to the parameter P_EMPNO , means the employee with EMPNO 7900 will get an increase of salary by 10% .

Example 1

```
CREATE PROCEDURE increase_sal (p_empno NUMBER)
IS
BEGIN
    UPDATE emp
    SET sal = sal + (sal * .10)
    WHERE  empno = p_empno;
END;
/
```
Output
PL/SQL Procedure successfully completed

Executing from ISQL* PLUS

SQL>EXECUTE increase_sal(7900);
Output
PL/SQL Procedure successfully completed

Note: that the parameter P_EMPNO in the procedure header is called formal parameter while the value 7900 which is assigned to the procedure when calling it as EXECUTE increase_sal(7900); is called actual parameter.
If value is not provided for the actual parameters then the error is raised, for example we cannot call the procedure as

EXECUTE increase_sal;

Default value can be provided for the formal parameters, in this case it is not necessary to have an actual parameter against that formal parameter, In the following example the DEFAULT value for the actual parameter is 8888 so when calling the procedure if the actual parameter is not specified then the procedure will Execute with the default value of the actual parameter instead of giving an error. Because the value is not provided when calling the procedure so the salary of the employee 8888 will increase because of default value.

For example

```
CREATE PROCEDURE increase_sal (p_empno NUMBER DEFAULT 8888)
IS
BEGIN
   UPDATE emp
   SET sal = sal + (sal * .10)
   WHERE  empno = p_empno;
END;
/
```
Output
PL/SQL Procedure successfully completed

Executing from ISQL* PLUS

SQL>EXECUTE increase_sal;
Output
PL/SQL Procedure successfully completed

Note: that the default value can be only of the Data type of the corresponding actual parameter, as in the above example the P_EMPNO is of number data type so the DEFAULT value can be of number data type only.

Host or bind variables

Host variables are the variables of the environment where procedure is invoked like Oracle Forms, Oracle Reports, ISQL* PLUS etc
Host variables are required to get the value of OUT or IN OUT parameters in the procedure or to get the value returned by the function, host variables are prefixed by 'G' in PL/SQL.

In PL/SQL host variables are defined as

Syntax

VARIABLE variable_name Data type[Lenth for Varchar2]

Example 1

SQL>VARIABLE g_get_val NUMBER
Or
SQL>VARIABLE g_get_name varchar2(30);

Note: that length is provided only for VARCHAR2 data type. Host variables in Pl/SQL are printed by PRINT keyword as following

SQL>PRINT g_get_val

Example 2

```
CREATE PROCEDURE increase_sal (p_empno NUMBER)
IS
BEGIN
   UPDATE emp
   SET sal = sal + (sal * .10)
   WHERE  empno = p_empno;
END;
/
```
Output
PL/SQL Procedure successfully completed

Executing from ISQL* PLUS
```
SQL> EXECUTE increase_sal(7900);
```
Output
PL/SQL Procedure successfully completed

In the following example the procedure with OUT parameter is created, this procedure convert_km_m will convert Kilo meters to meters. One actual parameter is given a KM value against formal parameter P_KM to take the value into the procedure and one actual parameter is defined to take the value of formal parameter p_m from procedure.
When procedure is execute as

```
EXECUTE convert_km_m(1,:g_meters);
```

The procedure multiplies 1 with 1000 and assigns this to P_M, P_M has OUT mode so it will take the value outside of the procedure.

There should be an actual variable (host variable) to take the value of OUT parameter with the same data type as of formal parameter, in the following example host variable G_METER of ISQL*Plus is defined, G_METER will get the value and PRINT command will print its output.

Example 2

```
CREATE OR REPLACE PROCEDURE convert_km_m (p_km IN NUMBER, p_m OUT NUMBER)
IS
BEGIN
   p_m     := p_km * 1000;
END;
/
```
Output
PL/SQL procedure successfully completed

SQL>variable g_meters NUMBER
SQL>EXECUTE convert_km_m(1,:g_meters);
SQL>PRINT g_meters
Output
1000

Note: that the variable G_METER is prefixed with colon when called in the EXECUTE statement because the variable is of ISQL*Plus and EXECUTE command is a SQL command, when we use the host variable in Print command the prefix colon is not required.

We can also call one procedure from other procedure, PL/SQL Block, trigger, Function or Package. We can call the above procedure in PL/SQL block as

```
DECLARE
   v_kilo_meters     NUMBER (4)  := &p_km;
   v_meters          NUMBER (6);
BEGIN
   convert_km_m (v_kilo_meters, v_meters);
   DBMS_OUTPUT.put_line (   v_kilo_meters
                        || ' km will be equal to '
                        || v_meters
                        || ' m'
                        );
END;
/Output
```
1 km will be equal to 1000 m
PL/SQL procedure successfully completed
Note that in the above PL/SQL block the variable v_meters is local variable.

The same functionality can be achieved by the IN OUT parameter, because the two parameters are of same data type so instead of two parameters one parameter of IN OUT mode can do this functionality , as IN OUT parameter takes a values into the procedure and after performing some calculation can return the value with the same parameter .

The following example is the replica of the previous, instead of two parameters one parameter of IN OUT mode is used to pass the value into and out of the procedure.

Drop the procedure convert_km_m and recreate the procedure with one parameter as of following,
To drop the procedure use the following command

```
DROP PROCEDURE convert_km_m
```

This command will drop the procedure convert_km_m and the procedure can be recreated or just use OR REPLACE keyword when creating a procedure which will automatically drop the previous procedure and recreate it, if there is not any previous procedure then a new procedure is created, so it is always a good practice to use OR REPLACE keyword as of following example

Example

```
CREATE OR REPLACE PROCEDURE convert_km_m (p_km_m IN OUT NUMBER)
IS
BEGIN
    p_km_m      := p_km_m * 1000;
END;
/
```
Output
PL/SQL procedure successfully completed
SQL>variable meters NUMBER:=1;
SQL>EXECUTE convert_km_m(:meters);
Output
1000

Note: that the parameter NUMBER is given a value of 1 and passed into the procedure, an printed the returned value by the same parameter.
Variable passed for IN OUT parameter should always be initialized.

Invoking a procedure from another procedure

You can invoke one procedure from another procedure; the following example invokes the previous procedure to calculate the Meters of first 10 Kilometers as

Example 1

```
CREATE OR REPLACE PROCEDURE calculate_meters
IS
   v_meters    NUMBER (6);
BEGIN
   FOR i IN 1 .. 10
   LOOP
      v_meters     := i;
      convert_km_m (v_meters);
      DBMS_OUTPUT.put_line (i || ' KM = ' || v_meters || ' M');
   END LOOP;
END;
```

Output
1 KM = 1000 M
2 KM = 2000 M
3 KM = 3000 M
4 KM = 4000 M

....

....

9 KM = 9000 M
10 KM = 10000 M
PLSQL procedure successfully completed

EXCEPTION handling with procedures

Exception handling can be done in Procedure similarly as in PL/SQL block as in the following example

The procedure below takes employee number as input parameter and selects the data of the employee and prints it, as there is a SELECT statement so if the employee doesn't exists then the EXCEPTION NO_DATA_FOUND will raise, Exception handler is used to handle this exception

Example 1

```
CREATE OR REPLACE PROCEDURE get_info (p_empno NUMBER)
IS
    v_sal     NUMBER (6);
    v_name    VARCHAR2 (30);
BEGIN
    SELECT ename,
           sal
    INTO   v_name,
           v_sal
    FROM   emp
    WHERE  empno = p_empno;

    DBMS_OUTPUT.put_line (v_name || ' ' || TO_NUMBER (v_sal));
EXCEPTION
    WHEN NO_DATA_FOUND
    THEN
        DBMS_OUTPUT.put_line ('Employee does not exists');
        NULL;
END;
/
```
Output
PL/SQL procedure successfully completed

```
BEGIN
    get_info (799999);
END;
/
```
Output
Employee does not exists

If Exception section is not provided in the procedure then the exception terminates the procedure and comes in the calling PL/SQL block , If EXCEPTION section is provided in the calling block the exception is trapped else it gives an error.

In the following example the Exception section is replaced from the procedure, Exception will be unhandled in the called procedure and in the calling block so an unhandled error occurs.

Note: that after the exception occurred in the SELECT statement it by passed the DBMS_OUTPUT.PUT_LINE procedure and in the calling PL/SQL block it also bypassed the DBMS_OUTPUT.PUT_LINE procedure which comes just after the procedure call.

Example 2

```
CREATE OR REPLACE PROCEDURE get_info (p_empno NUMBER)
IS
    v_sal     NUMBER (4);
    v_name    VARCHAR2 (30);
BEGIN
    SELECT ename,
           sal
    INTO   v_name,
           v_sal
    FROM   emp
    WHERE  empno = p_empno;

    DBMS_OUTPUT.put_line (v_name || ' ' || TO_NUMBER (v_sal));
END;
/
```

Output
PL/SQL procedure successfully completed

```
BEGIN
    get_info (7999);
    DBMS_OUTPUT.put_line ('Statement after Procedure');
END;
/
```
Output
ORA-01403: no data found
ORA-06512: at "SCOTT.GET_INFO", line 6
ORA-06512: at line 2

In the following example the error is handled in the calling PL/SQL block , but the Exception originally raised in the select statement of the called procedure get_info so it bypassed all other statements after select statement and searched for the Exception section, the EXCEPTION section is not defined in the called procedure so the Exception came in the calling PL/SQL block, it bypassed the DBMS_OUTPUT.PUT_LINE procedure and searched the EXCEPTION section , EXCEPTION section is defined for the PL/SQL block so the Exception is handled.

The DBMS_OUTPUT.PUT_LINE before procedure call, executes only , because exception was not raised till the time.

Example 3

```
CREATE OR REPLACE PROCEDURE get_info (p_empno NUMBER)
IS
    v_sal    NUMBER (4);
    v_name   VARCHAR2 (30);
BEGIN
    SELECT ename,
           sal
    INTO   v_name,
           v_sal
    FROM   emp
    WHERE  empno = p_empno;

    DBMS_OUTPUT.put_line (v_name || ' ' || TO_NUMBER (v_sal));
END;
/
```

Output
PL/SQL procedure successfully completed

```
BEGIN
    DBMS_OUTPUT.put_line ('Statement before Procedure call');
    get_info (7999);
    DBMS_OUTPUT.put_line ('Statement after Procedure call');
EXCEPTION
    WHEN NO_DATA_FOUND
    THEN
        DBMS_OUTPUT.put_line ('Employee does not exists');
END;
/
```
Output

Statement before Procedure call

Employee does not exists

PL/SQL procedure successfully completed.

Compile time warnings

You can now check the compile time warnings of a procedure(Oracle 11g feature), function or package by setting the PLSQL_WARNING parameter, The warning types are categorized as ALL, SEVERE, INFORMATIONAL and PERFORMACE. You can also convert a warning into error that halts the compilation. Before compiling the procedure the PLSQL_WARNING parameter is ENABLE which is DISABLED by default, You can get the current value of the PLSQL_WARINING parameter by using DMBS_WARNING.GET_WARNING_SETTING_STRING( ),
 if there are any compilation warnings you can see these by using SHOW ERRORS.

The following example shows that there is a condition in the IF statement that 'IF 1=1 THEN' which will always yield 'TRUE' so the ELSE part of the statement will never execute hence the warning is shown that the code is unreachable.

Example 1

```
SELECT dbms_warning.get_warning_setting_string ()
FROM    DUAL;
/
Output
DISABLED

ALTER SESSION SET plsql_warnings='ENABLE:ALL';
Output
SESSION ALTERED


SELECT dbms_warning.get_warning_setting_string ()
FROM    DUAL;
/
Output
ENABLED


CREATE OR REPLACE PROCEDURE test_warnings
AS
   l_dummy     VARCHAR2 (10) := '1';
BEGIN
   IF 1 = 1
   THEN
      SELECT '2'
      INTO    l_dummy
      FROM    DUAL;
   ELSE
      raise_application_error (-20000, 'l_dummy != 1!');

END IF;
END;
```

/
SP2-0804: Procedure created with compilation warnings

SHOW ERRORS

Errors for PROCEDURE TEST_WARNINGS:
LINE/COL ERROR

-------- ----------------------------
9/5   PLW-06002: Unreachable code

NOTE: Here the procedure is created and compiled; you can also compile the procedure only, if it is already created as following.

```
ALTER  PROCEDURE test_warnings COMPILE;
```

You can also set the PLSQL_WARNING parameter only for one procedure while compiling it as following

```
ALTER PROCEDURE test_warnings COMPILE    PLSQL_WARNING='ENABLE: PERFORMAANCE';
```

You can also code if you want to hear about 'SEVERE' warning don't want to hear about 'PERFORMANCE' and want plw-06002 warning to produce error that Should halt compilation as following

```
ALTER SESSION SET
PLSQL_WARNING='ENABLE:SEVERE','DISABLE:PERFORMANCE','ERROR:06002';
```

Dropping a procedure

Syntax
```
DROP PROCEDURE procedure_name
```

Example

```
DROP PROCEDURE raise_salary;
```
Output
Procedure dropped

Summary

In this lesson you have learned about the procedure that procedure is a named PL/SQL block that perform some action, benefits of a procedure are Modularity, reusability, maintainability and extensibility, how to create a procedure, what are parameters, Parameter Modes (IN, OUT, IN OUT), invoking procedure with different parameter modes, Exception handling with procedure, compile time warnings that compile time warnings tell the user about the unusual behavior of the program units and drooping a procedure.

Exercise

1. Create a procedure that should accept two parameter of IN mode, one should take EMPNO and other should take INCREAMENT_AMOUNT, the procedure should raise the salary according to the passed parameters of the particular employee.

2. Create a procedure that should take two parameters, P_DEPTNO of IN mode to take the DEPNO and P_SAL of OUT mode to take the maximum salary, the procedure should select the max salary of the employee in particular department (P_DEPTNO) and return through P_SAL parameter, also writer code to call this procedure at SQL prompt.

3. Modify the above procedure, instead of two parameters create one parameter to take the DEPTNO and return the maximum salary, also writer code to call this procedure at SQL prompt and in the PL/SQL block.

4. Following is the procedure get_info which get the employee's name and SAL and following is a PL/SQL block which call the procedure and prints one message 'Calling Procedure', when the procedure is called against nonexistent employee message 'Employee does not exits' comes, Why the message in the calling program is not showing and what should be done to execute the calling program successfully and print the message.

```
CREATE OR REPLACE PROCEDURE get_info (p_empno NUMBER)
IS
    v_sal      NUMBER (6);
    v_name     VARCHAR2 (30);
BEGIN
    SELECT ename,
           sal
    INTO   v_name,
           v_sal
    FROM   emp
    WHERE  empno = p_empno;

    DBMS_OUTPUT.put_line (v_name || ' ' || TO_NUMBER (v_sal)); END;
```

PROCEDURES

```
BEGIN
    get_info (79);
    DBMS_OUTPUT.put_line ('CALLING PROCEDURE');
EXCEPTION
    WHEN NO_DATA_FOUND
    THEN
        DBMS_OUTPUT.put_line ('Employee does not exists');
END;
```

5. What is wrong with the following example

```
CREATE OR REPLACE PROCEDURE get_info (p_empno NUMBER)
IS
    v_sal     NUMBER (6);
    v_name    VARCHAR2 (30);
BEGIN
    p_empno     := '7900';

    SELECT ename,
           sal
    INTO   v_name,
           v_sal
    FROM   emp
    WHERE  empno = p_empno;

    DBMS_OUTPUT.put_line (v_name || ' ' || TO_NUMBER (v_sal));
END;
/
```

13 FUNCTIONS

In this chapter you will learn about

What is a function?
Difference between a procedure and function
Create a function
User defined function with SQL expressions
Drop a function

What is a Function?

A function is a named PL/SQL block that returns a value, there is not much difference between a procedure and a function, the only difference is that function is executed as part of an expression and function must return a value, whereas a procedure can return 0 or more values and is executed as statement. A function must have a return clause in the header and at least one return statement in the executable section. A function is stored in the data base as schema object, and can be called anywhere the functionality is required, thus improves reusability and function can be extended by changing the code in the function body thus improves maintainability.

Creating a function

Syntax

CREATE [OR REPLACE] FUNCTION name
[(parameter1 [MODE] datatype1,
Parameter2 [MODE] datatype2…..)]

RETURN datatype

IS|AS

BEGIN
Statement 1;
Statement 2;
RETURN value;
EXCEPTION
--Exception Handeling
END [name];

OR REPLACE keyword drops the object if it already exists, FUNCTION key identifies that the object which is giong to generate is a function, name gives a name to the function, [(parameter1 [MODE] datatype1)] identifies the parameters their MODE and there data type, RETURN statement in the executable section identifies that the value to be returned.

The value in the RETURN statement in the executable section should be of the same data type as the RETURN clause in the header.

Note: that the parameter modes OUT and IN OUT can be used with a function but they are not recommended.

The following example creates a simple function conv_km_m that converts Kilo meters to meters, parameter km is a parameter of type NUMBER and mode IN which is used to take the value which needs to be converted, RETURN NUMBER indicates that returned value of meters will be of NUMBER data type.

RETURN statement in the executable section simply multiplies KM parameter's value by 1000 to convert it into meters and returns it.

Example 1

```
CREATE OR REPLACE FUNCTION conv_km_m (km NUMBER)
    RETURN NUMBER
IS
BEGIN
--Converts Km to meters by multiply by 1000 and RETURN is used to return the
value
    RETURN (km * 1000);
END;
/
```
Output
PL/SQL procedure successfully completed

Following is the example of executing the above function by ISQL* Plus.

Note: that you can use SHOW ERRORS to see compilation errors if the function is created with errors.

VARIABLE keyword created a bind variable G_METERS of NUMBER data type, to take the returned value of the function, EXECUTE command executes the function by giving value 1 to the function and takes the returned value into the bind variable G_METERS.

PRINT command prints the value of the bind variable G_METERS.

VARIABLE g_meters NUMBER
EXECUTE :g_meters=conv_km_m(1);
PRINT g_meters
Output
1000

The above function is called in the PL/SQL blocks as following; the following PL/SQL block declares a variable V_KM as of NUMBER data type and takes its value through substitution variable, V_METERS is a variable of NUMBER data type to take the returned value.
In the executable section the function is called by giving the value of V_KM and returned value is stored into V_METERS and value is printed by using DBMS_OUTPUT.PUT_LINE procedure.

```
DECLARE
    v_km        NUMBER := &km;
    v_meters    NUMBER;
BEGIN
    v_meters    := conv_km_m (v_km);
    DBMS_OUTPUT.put_line (v_km || ' kilo meters are equal to  ' || v_meters);
END;
/
```

Output
2 kilo meters are equal to 2000 meters
PL/SQL procedure successfully completed

User defined function with SQL expressions

Functions can extend SQL, where there are complex, awkward activities are involved with SQL. When functions are used in where clause to filter data they greatly improve efficiency as oppose to filter the data in the application.
The following example creates a function which accepts a value and increase the value by 10% and returns, this function is used to improve the salaries of employee in SQL expressions as

Example 1

```
CREATE OR REPLACE FUNCTION inc_sal (p_sal NUMBER)
    RETURN NUMBER
IS
BEGIN
    RETURN (p_sal + (p_sal * .1));
END;
/
```
Output ...Function created

```
SELECT empno,
```

```
        ename,
        sal,
        inc_sal (sal) after_increment
FROM    emp
/
```
Output

EMPNO ENAME	SAL	AFTER_INCREMENT
7369 SMITHXDCF	880.11	968.121
7499 ALLEN	1600	1760
7521 WARD	1250	1375

In SQL you can call user defined functions in SELECT list of select command, conditions of where and having clauses, in order by, connect by, start with, group by clause, values clause of insert statement, and in update statement in set clause.

```
SELECT empno,
        ename,
        sal,
        inc_sal (sal) after_increment
FROM    emp
WHERE   sal > (SELECT MAX (inc_sal (sal))
                FROM    emp
                WHERE   deptno = 10)
/
```
Output

EMPNO ENAME	SAL	AFTER_INCREMENT
7900 JAMES	17600	19360

Note: Output can be different according to the data in EMP tables

There are some restrictions in calling functions from SQL Expressions
A function must follow following rules to be callable from SQL Expression

1. It should be a stored function
2. It should accept only IN parameters
3. It should have valid SQL data types in parameters not PL/SQL specific type like collections.
4. It should not contain any DML statement
5. It should not perform DML or it should not query the table if this function is used in UPDATE/DELETE statement of the same table otherwise "Table is mutating" error will rise.
6. It should not contain COMMIT, ROLLBAK, SAVPOINT statements

As shown in the following example, the function is inserting a record into EMP table so when same function is used in Update statement of the same table the error is raised.

Example 2

```
CREATE OR REPLACE FUNCTION insert_emp (p_val NUMBER)
    RETURN NUMBER
IS
BEGIN
    INSERT INTO emp
                (empno,
                 ename,
                 deptno
                )
    VALUES      (101,
                 'AQSA',
                 10
                );

    RETURN (p_val * .1);
END;
/
OUTPUT
PLSQL procedure successfully completed

UPDATE emp
SET sal = insert_emp (sal)
WHERE   empno = 7900
/
OUTPUT
SET sal=INSERT_emp(sal)
          *
ERROR at line 2:
ORA-04091: table SCOTT.EMP is mutating, trigger/function may not see it
ORA-06512: at "SCOTT.INSERT_EMP", line 5
```

Droping Function

Syntax
DROP FUNCTION function_name;

Example 1

```
DROP FUNCTION insert_emp
/
Output
Function dropped
```

Summary

In this chapter you have learned that Function compute a value and returns, how to invoke a function from ISQL PLUS and PL/SQL block, how the functions are called from SQL statement and what are the restrictions in calling a function from SQL statements.

Exercise

1. Create a function that take the EMPNO as input parameter and returns the salary of the employee, pass the EMPNO of any employee and print the returned salary, use both ISQL* Plus and PL/SQL blocks to call the function.

2. create a function that should take two parameters, one should be value other should be unit, if the unit will be 'M' then functions will accept kilometers and will return meters and if the unit is 'F' the function will accept Celsius as value an will return the Fahrenheit as temperature else if the unit is any other value then function will return null;

3. Create a function that should accept the DOB of a user and return the number of days , number of weeks or number of years since his/her DOB, a parameter should be provided to select the criteria, 'D' for number of days, 'W' for weeks, 'Y' for years.

    For example the function is called as `cal_age_days (TO_DATE ('31-01- 1983', 'dd-mm-rrrr'), 'Y')` the function should return the age of the person in years.

4. Why the error comes when the following function is called in the following query

```
CREATE OR REPLACE FUNCTION upd_emp (p_emp NUMBER)
    RETURN NUMBER
IS
BEGIN
    UPDATE emp
    SET sal = sal + (sal * .10)
    WHERE  empno = p_emp;

    RETURN (0);
END;
/


SELECT upd_emp (empno)
FROM   emp;
/
```

14 SUBPROGRAMS MANAGEMENT

In this chapter you will learn about

Difference between system privileges and object privileges
Using views of data dictionary to manage stored objects
Difference between invokers rights and definers rights

Difference between system privilege and object privilege

Systems privilege are assigned by the user SYSTEM or SYS, privileges that use the word CRATE or ANY **are** system privileges; For example GRANT ALTER ANY TABLE TO farhan; Object privileges are associated with specific object, contain object name and are assigned by the owner of the object, for example Scott user grants EXECUTE privilege to farhan as

```
GRANT EXECUTE ON emp_select TO farhan;
```

Object privileges include the name of the object as emp_select in above statement
To create any procedure you should have SYSTEM privilege CREATE ANY PROCEDURE, once you have created your procedure you are not required to have any privilege to ALTER or drop that procedure. If any user has the SYSTEM privilege EXECUTE ANY PROCEDURE, he can execute any procedure else he should have the object privilege to execute any particular Procedure.

Note: that the keyword PROCEDURE is used for stored procedures, functions, and packages.

Using views of data dictionary to manage stored objects

1. USER_OBJECTS data dictionary view

User_object contain information about all the objects in one schema user_objects view has following columns

Object_name	identifies the name of the object
Object_id	internal identifier for the object
Object_type	object type such as procedure, function, package, trigger, package body
Last_ddl_time	date when the object was last modified
Status	status can be valid or invalid

You can also test All_objects and Dba_object to view the owner information; both contain one additional column Owner.

For example you want to know about all the procedures and functions in Scott schema, you can get the information as following

Example 1

```
SELECT     object_name,
           object_type
FROM       user_objects
WHERE      object_type IN ('PROCEDURE', 'FUNCTION')
ORDER BY object_name
/
```
Output
OBJECT_NAME   OBJECT_TYPE
MY_CONVERTOR   FUNCTION
....

You can also check DBA_OBJECT S and ALL_OBJECTS each of which contain one additional column for the owner of the object.

2. USER_SOURCE data dictionary view

This data dictionary view is used to get the source code of procedures, functions and packages, its columns are specified as following

Name   Object name
Type   Procedure, Function, Package, Package body
Line   Line number of the source code
Text   Text of the source code

You can also test All_objects and Dba_object to view the owner information; both contain one additional column Owner.
In the following example source code of the procedure 'MY_CONVERTOR' is shown

Example 1

```
SELECT text
FROM   user_source
WHERE  NAME = 'MY_CONVERTOR'
/
```
Output

TEXT

FUNCTION my_convertor(p_value NUMBER,p_unit varchar2)
RETURN VARCHAR2
IS
BEGIN
If p_unit='M' THEN
RETURN(TO_CHAR(P_VALUE)||'KM= '||TO_CHAR(P_VALUE*1000)||' meters');
ELSIF p_unit='F' THEN
return((9/5)*p_value+32);
ELSE
RETURN NULL;
END IF;

TEXT

END;

You can also check DBA_OBJECT S and ALL_OBJECTS each of which contains one additional column for the owner of the object.

Difference between invokers rights and definers rights

By default the procedure is executed under the security privileges of its creator (definer).
For example Scott create a procedure emp_select, the procedure selects the emp table and prints the information, scott grants Execute Privilage on emp_select to user Farhan, now though the user Farhan has not select privialge on emp table yet he can Execute procedure which is selecting the EMP table because the procedure by default executes under the security privileges of the definer.

Example 1

LOGIN as \as sysdba

```
CREATE USER farhan IDENTIFIED BY farhan;
```

LOGOUT

LOGIN to Scott and create following procedure

```
CREATE OR REPLACE PROCEDURE emp_select (p_empno NUMBER)
IS
   ename     VARCHAR2 (30);
BEGIN
   SELECT ename
   INTO   ename
   FROM   emp
   WHERE  empno = p_empno;

   DBMS_OUTPUT.put_line (ename);
END;
/
```
Output
PL/SQL procedure successfully completed

```
GRANT EXECUTE ON emp_select TO farhan;
```

Output
GRANT SUCCEED

Now logout from Scott and login to farhan and execute the procedure

```
SET SERVEROUTPUT ON
EXECUTE emp_select(7900);
```
Output
JAMES

The procedure executed successfully, now create the procedure as following in Scott's schema

```
CREATE OR REPLACE PROCEDURE emp_select (p_empno NUMBER)
AUTHID CURRENT_USER
IS
    ename     VARCHAR2 (30);
BEGIN
    SELECT ename
    INTO   ename
    FROM   emp
    WHERE  empno = p_empno;

    DBMS_OUTPUT.put_line (ename);
END;
/
```
Output
PL/SQL procedure successfully completed

Grant the execute privilege on procedure to farhan and execute the procedure in farhan's schema in similar way, This time the procedure will give an error because all the objects in the procedure will execute under the security privilege of the user farhan, farhan has not select privilege on EMP table so the procedure will not execute.
Though the default functionality is that the procedure executes under the security privileges of the definer, you can also write "AUTHID DEFINER" when creating procedure for your satisfaction.

Summary

In this chapter your have learned the difference between System privileges and Object privileges', How to use data dictionary views to get information about the program units, and what is the difference between invoker's rights and definer's rights.

Exercise

1. The following procedure is created in 'SCOTT' schema, while 'FARHAN' has not any privilege on EMP table, will 'FARHAN' be able to execute the procedure? If not then what is the solution?

```
CREATE OR REPLACE PROCEDURE emp_procedure (p_empno NUMBER)
AUTHID CURRENT_USER;
IS
   v_ename    VARCHAR2 (30);
BEGIN
   SELECT ename
   INTO    v_ename
   FROM    emp
   WHERE   empno = p_empno;
END;
```

2. What is the difference between following two procedures

```
CREATE OR REPLACE PROCEDURE emp_procedure (p_empno NUMBER)
IS
   v_ename    VARCHAR2 (30);
BEGIN
   SELECT ename
   INTO    v_ename
   FROM    emp
   WHERE   empno = p_empno;
END;
```

```
CREATE OR REPLACE PROCEDURE emp_procedure (p_empno NUMBER)
AUTHID CURRENT_USER;
IS
   v_ename    VARCHAR2 (30);
BEGIN
   SELECT ename
   INTO    v_ename
   FROM    emp
   WHERE   empno = p_empno;
END;
```

3. How the text of a procedure emp_procedure can be seen?

4. How can you see the objects of any schema?

15 PACKAGES

In this chapter you will learn about

What is a package?
Package specification
Create package specification
Package body
Create package body
Calling a package
A body less package
Overloading with packaged program units
Creating one time only procedure
Declare PL/SQL composite data types in a package
Restrictions on packaged functions used in SQL

What is a package?

A package is just like a container which bundles procedures, functions, cursors, variables and types. The greatest benefit of a package is that when any content of the package is first called into user's schema all the package is loaded into the user's local memory so further calls read only from the local memory hence network traffic is reduced and response time is increased, another benefit is that you can gather all the related program units in one container.

A Package has two parts specification and body.
Package specification contains headers of program units, variables, cursors, type which are global, package body contains implementation of program units that are declared in package specification, if the program unit is used only within package body then no need to declare it in the specification just create it in the package body(private package).
Program units, variables, cursors, types only created in the package body are called private and can be called only from the package body thus improving security.
If Package specification contains only variables and types then there is no need to create package body. In the package you can overload program units, explained later in this chapter.

Package Specification

Syntax

CREATE OR REPLACE PACKAGE package_name
IS
[Declaration of variables and types]
[Declaration of program units]
[Declaration of Cursors]
END[Package_name];

Anything created in the package specification is called global and can be called from outside the package.
Package specification contains only the header of the program units, if any program unit is required in the package body only, then no need to declare it in the specification section.

Creation of Package specification

The following example creates a package specification with one variable and one function.
As there is function header only in the specification so its implementation is done in the package body.

Example 1

```
CREATE OR REPLACE PACKAGE pkg_emp_info
IS
   v_variable   NUMBER (10);

   FUNCTION emp_manager (p_empno NUMBER)
      RETURN VARCHAR2;
END;
/

Output
PL/SQL procedure successfully completed
```

Package Body

Syntax

CREATE OR REPLACE PACKAGE BODY package_name
IS
[Declaration of private variables and types]
[Implementation of Global program units||creation of private program units]
[Implimentation of Cursors]
END[Package_name];

Package body syntax contains an extra keyword BODY, Package body is required to implement the program units, cursors that are global.
Variables, constants, types, cursors and program units declared in package body only are called private and cannot be called from outside the package.

Creation of package body

Package body is created with additional BODY keyword.
In the following example the package body is created with one function.
As the function was declared in the package specification so the function is a global function, means it can be called from other external objects, the function simply returns the manager name of the employee; the EMP_NO is passed through parameter.
Note: that the function header should be same in package body as it is in the package specification for the same function.
Oracle server stores the package specification and package body separately in the database so you can change one without affecting the other.
If the function is private then no need to declare it in the package specification.

Example 1

```
CREATE OR REPLACE PACKAGE BODY pkg_emp_info
IS
   FUNCTION emp_manager (p_empno NUMBER)
      RETURN VARCHAR2
   IS
      v_mgr    VARCHAR2 (20);
   BEGIN
      SELECT m.ename manager
      INTO   v_mgr

      FROM   emp e, emp m
      WHERE  e.mgr = m.empno AND e.empno = p_empno;
```

```
        RETURN v_mgr;
    EXCEPTION
        WHEN NO_DATA_FOUND
        THEN
            raise_application_error (-20009, 'Please enter a valid employee');
    END;
END;
/
```

Out put
PL/SQL procedure successfully complete

Calling a package construct

The above packaged function can be called from ISQL*PLUS as following

```
VARIABLE g_mang VARCHAR2(30)
EXECUTE g_mang:=pkg_emp_info.emp_manager(7566);
PRINT g_mang
```

Output
KING

If the package is in different schema then prefix the schema name as

```
VARIABLE g_mang VARCHAR2(30)
EXECUTE g_mang:=scott.pkg_emp_info.emp_manager(7566);
PRINT g_mang
```

Or Test the packaged function with the following Select Statement in ISQL*PLUS

```
SELECT pkg_emp_info.emp_manager (7566)
FROM    DUAL;
/
```

Output
KINGS

In the following example the package is created with one variable, one function and one procedure. The variable is declared in the package specification, The variables declared in the package can be used as an alternative of Global variable. As mentioned earlier that package specification contain only headers of program units(procedures, functions) so only headers are declared of procedure give_comm and function cal_comm in the specification.

In the package body there is a private function check_sal which checks the employee's salary, if the salary is greater than 10000 the function returns FALSE else TRUE, means this function will be used to validate that the employee's salary should be less than 10000 to get the commission.

The function give_comm update the salary of the specified employee by the percent passed by the user through P_COMM parameter, It validate that either employee is eligible of getting commission or not by calling the function check_sal.

The function Check_sal is created in the package body only (private) because it is required in the package body only. The function cal_comm returns 10 percent of the salary of the employee specified. In the exception section conditions are specified to handle the exceptions, especially when invalid employee is passed.

Because all the contents of the package are about the employee so they are kept in one package.

Example 2

```
CREATE OR REPLACE PACKAGE emp_package
IS
    v_global    NUMBER (10);

    PROCEDURE give_comm (p_empno NUMBER, p_comm NUMBER);

    FUNCTION cal_comm (p_empno NUMBER)
        RETURN NUMBER;
END;

--Package body
CREATE OR REPLACE PACKAGE BODY emp_package
IS
    FUNCTION check_sal (p_empno NUMBER)
        RETURN BOOLEAN
    IS
        v_sal    NUMBER;
    BEGIN
        SELECT sal
        INTO   v_sal
        FROM   emp
        WHERE  empno = p_empno;

        IF v_sal > 10000
        THEN
            RETURN FALSE;

ELSE
        RETURN TRUE;
```

```
            END IF;
      EXCEPTION
         WHEN NO_DATA_FOUND
         THEN
             raise_application_error (-20014, 'Employee does not exists');
      END;

      PROCEDURE give_comm (p_empno NUMBER, p_comm NUMBER)
      IS
      BEGIN
         IF check_sal (p_empno)
         THEN
             UPDATE emp
             SET sal = round(sal + (sal*(p_comm / 100)))
             WHERE  empno = p_empno;
         ELSE
             raise_application_error (-20013,
                                   'Employee is not elgible of commision'
                                  );
         END IF;
      END;

      FUNCTION cal_comm (p_empno NUMBER)
         RETURN NUMBER
      IS
         v_sal    NUMBER;
      BEGIN
         SELECT sal
         INTO    v_sal
         FROM    emp
         WHERE   empno = p_empno;

         RETURN (v_sal * 0.1);
      EXCEPTION
         WHEN NO_DATA_FOUND
         THEN
             raise_application_error (-20011, 'Emp does not exist');
         WHEN OTHERS
         THEN
             raise_application_error (-20012, 'Some Unhandled exception');
      END;
END;
/
```

Note: A package itself cannot be invoked, parameterized or nested.

To check the 10% commission of each employee use following

```
--returns 10% comm of each emp
SELECT sal,
       emp_package.cal_comm (empno) comm
FROM   emp;
/
```

```
Output
    SAL     COMM
---------- ----------
   880.11   88.011
     1600     160
     1250     125
```

To check the procedure give_comm use the following statements
First check any employee's salary that is lower than 8000 as

```
SELECT sal
FROM   emp
WHERE  empno = 7521;
/
Output
1250
```

Execute the procedure

```
exec emp_package.give_comm(7521,20);
```

Output
PL/SQL procedure successfully completed

Just select the employee's salary again as

```
SELECT sal
FROM   emp
WHERE  empno = 7521;
/
Output
1500
```

A body less package

If the package specification does not contain procedure or function then package body is not required.
The following example creates a package which converts units like Mile to Kilo meter.
The variables declared in the example are called public or global variables that exist for the duration of the user session and can be used as an alternative of global variables.

Example 1

```
CREATE OR REPLACE PACKAGE convert_units
IS
    mile_2_kilo    CONSTANT NUMBER := 1.6093;
    kilo_2_mile    CONSTANT NUMBER := 0.6214;
    yard_2_meter   CONSTANT NUMBER := 0.9144;
END convert_units;
/
```

```
EXECUTE DBMS_OUTPUT.PUT_LINE('15 miles= '||15*convert_units.mile_2_kilo||' km');
```

Output
15 miles= 24.1395 km
PL/SQL procedure successfully completed.

Drooping a package

Syntax
DROP PACKAGE package_name;
DROP PACKAGE BODY package_name;

DROP PACKAGE removes the package specification and package body, DROP PACKAGE BODY removes only the package body.

Example 1

```
DROP PACKAGE convert_units
/
Output
Packaged dropped
```

Overloading

Multiple functions and procedures with the same name but different parameters is called overloading. Oracle call the specific function or procedure which have the same name by realizing the parameters passed to it. The example of the overloading is built in functions as to_number, to_char, to_date etc. for instance to_char can be called by

to_char('9999'); or to_char(SYSDATE,'DDMMRR');

So as in the above example, if two or more functions or procedures are performing same functionality by accepting different parameters then logically their name should be same.
Indeed these are two separate functions with the same name but with different parameters.
The formal parameters should be different in name, number, order or data type family for the overloaded program units.

Overloading cannot be performed

1. If formal parameters are different in data types and that data types belong to same family as NUMBER and DECIMAL belong to the same family.

2. If formal parameters are different in sub types and that sub types belong to same family as VARCHAR and STRING are subtypes of VARCHAR2.

3. Two functions that are different in RETURN type only
NOTE: The above restrictions apply if the names of the parameters are also same.

The following example creates overloaded procedures, which are used to increase the employee's salary, if the procedure is called with only EMPNO parameter passed to it then the salary of the employee will be increased by 10%, and if the procedure is called with the EMPNO and P_INC PARAMTERS passed to it then salary will increase according to the amount passed THROUGHT P_INC parameter.

Example 1

```
--Overloaded package
--Increase the emp sal according to the parameters passed
CREATE OR REPLACE PACKAGE ol_pkg
IS
    PROCEDURE raise_sal (p_emp NUMBER);
```

```
    PROCEDURE raise_sal (p_emp NUMBER, p_inc NUMBER);
END;
/
Output
Package created

--Overloaded package
--Increase the emp sal according to the parameters passed
CREATE OR REPLACE PACKAGE BODY ol_pkg
IS
    PROCEDURE raise_sal (p_emp NUMBER)
    IS
    BEGIN
       UPDATE emp
       SET sal = sal + (sal * .10)
       WHERE  empno = p_emp;
    END;

    PROCEDURE raise_sal (p_emp NUMBER, p_inc NUMBER)
    IS
    BEGIN
       UPDATE emp
       SET sal = sal+p_inc
       WHERE  empno = p_emp;
    END;
END;
/
Output
Package body created

Testing

EXEC ol_pkg2.raise_sal(7100);
Output
PL/SQL procedure successfully completed

EXEC ol_pkg2.raise_sal(7782,1200);
Output
PL/SQL procedure successfully completed
```

The employee with EMPNO 7100 will get a 10% increment and employee with EMPNO 7782 will get an increment of 1200.

Following example shows the procedures which cannot be overloaded

Example 2

```
--Overloaded package
--Increase the emp sal according to the parameters passed

CREATE OR REPLACE PACKAGE ol_pkg2
IS
    PROCEDURE raise_sal (p_emp NUMBER, p_inc INTEGER);

    PROCEDURE raise_sal (p_emp NUMBER, p_inc NUMBER);
END;
/

--Overloaded package
--Increase the emp sal according to the parameters passed

CREATE OR REPLACE PACKAGE BODY ol_pkg
IS
    PROCEDURE raise_sal (p_emp NUMBER)
    IS
    BEGIN
       UPDATE emp
       SET sal = sal + (sal * .10)
       WHERE  empno = p_emp;
    END;

    PROCEDURE raise_sal (p_emp NUMBER, p_inc NUMBER)
    IS
    BEGIN
       UPDATE emp
       SET sal = p_inc
       WHERE  empno = p_emp;
    END;
END;
/

EXEC ol_pkg2.raise_sal(7100,1000);
```
Output
*

ERROR at line 1:
ORA-06550: line 1, column 7:
PLS-00307: too many declarations of 'RAISE_SAL' match this call
ORA-06550: line 1, column 7:
PL/SQL: Statement ignored

Note: though the package created successfully, but failed to call the procedure, because two procedures are same except the data type of the second parameter, but the data type NUMBER and INTEGER belong to same family so and error will rise when calling the procedure.

Improved Overloading With Numeric Types in 10g

You can now overload subprograms that accept different type of numeric arguments.
 For example a number accepting BINARY_FLOAT might be faster, while a
 Function accepting BINARY_DOUBLE might provide more precision.
 Following is the example of overloading

Example 1

```
-- Create package specification.
CREATE OR REPLACE PACKAGE numeric_overload_test AS
     PROCEDURE overload_pro (p_number   NUMBER);
     PROCEDURE overload_pro (p_number   BINARY_FLOAT);
     PROCEDURE overload_pro (p_number   BINARY_DOUBLE);
END;
/
Output
Package created

CREATE OR REPLACE PACKAGE BODY numeric_overload_test AS
  PROCEDURE overload_pro (p_number   NUMBER) AS
  BEGIN
    DBMS_OUTPUT.put_line('Using NUMBER');
  END;

  PROCEDURE overload_pro (p_number   BINARY_FLOAT) AS
  BEGIN
    DBMS_OUTPUT.put_line('Using BINARY_FLOAT');
  END;

  PROCEDURE overload_pro (p_number   BINARY_DOUBLE) AS
  BEGIN
    DBMS_OUTPUT.put_line('Using BINARY_DOUBLE');
  END;
END;
/
Output
Package created
```

```
-- Test it.
SET SERVEROUTPUT ON
BEGIN
  numeric_overload_test. overload_pro (10);
  numeric_overload_test. overload_pro (10.1f);
  numeric_overload_test. overload_pro (10.1d);
END;
/
Output
Using NUMBER
Using BINARY_FLOAT
Using BINARY_DOUBLE
PL/SQL procedure successfully completed
```

Using forward declarations

In the package body if you call a private procedure or function(that is declared in the package body only) of the same package and the procedure or function is written after the place where you are calling , it is called forward referencing that PL/SQL does not allow, an identifier must be declared before using it.
In package body you can use forward referencing by declaring the header of procedure or function before the place where you are calling.

Not allowed

```
CREATE OR REPLACE PACKAGE BODY forward_ref
IS

PROCEDURE calling_proc
IS

Called_proc;
……………….
END;

PROCEDURE called_proc
IS
BEGIN

Statements1;
Statements2;
…………….

END;

END forward_ref;
```

Allowed

```
CREATE OR REPLACE PACKAGE BODY forward_ref
IS

PROCEDURE called_proc;  -- Forward reference
PROCEDURE calling_proc
IS
```

```
Called_proc;
………………
END;

PROCEDURE called_proc
IS
BEGIN

Statements1;
Statements2;
…………….

END;

END forward_ref;
```

Creating a onetime only procedure

A onetime only procedure executes only once when the package is first invoked within the user schema, you can set the values that need to be constant within a user schema.
A onetime only procedure in written at last in PACKAGE BODY without any END keyword.
Following example creates a onetime only procedure that will execute only once when the package is first invoked within the user schema and will get the name of the department where DEPTNO is equal to 10.

Example 1

```
Create or replace package onetime_pkg
Is
V_deptname VARCHAR2(30);
…………………………………
--all public procedures, functions and variables
END onetime_pkg;
/
CREATE OR REPLACE PACKAGE BODY onetime_pkg
IS
----declare or impliment all procedures, functions, cursors, variables

--one time only procedure
BEGIN
SELECT dname
Into v_deptname
From dept where dept=10;

END onetime_pkg;
/
```

NOTE: one time only procedure is without END keyword.

The following example creates a package with one function sal_greated_maxsal with accepts a parameter and compare its values with the maximum salary of the employee if the value is greater than it returns TRUE else FALSE.

The maximum salary is get in a private variable V_MAXSAL by onetime only procedure, check the procedure with the statement provided at last, look the maximum SAL and check the package, then update the maximum SAL and check, you will see that the maximum SAL will not be changed in the package because the package keeps the maximum SAL in the variable until the session terminates.

Example 1

```
--Package specification created
-- Function will get salary as parameter
-- and will compare it with maximum salary of the employees
-- and return true if the salary is greater the max salary

CREATE OR REPLACE PACKAGE onetime_pkg
IS
    v_deptname    VARCHAR2 (30);

    FUNCTION sal_greater_maxsal (p_sal NUMBER)
        RETURN BOOLEAN;
END onetime_pkg;
/
Output
Package created

-- Creation of the package body
-- maximum sal is fetched through onetime only procedure

CREATE OR REPLACE PACKAGE BODY onetime_pkg
IS
    v_maxsal    NUMBER (10);

    FUNCTION sal_greater_maxsal (p_sal NUMBER)
        RETURN BOOLEAN
    IS
    BEGIN
        IF p_sal > v_maxsal
        THEN
            RETURN TRUE;
        ELSE
            RETURN FALSE;
        END IF;
    END;
BEGIN
    SELECT MAX (sal)
    INTO   v_maxsal
    FROM   emp;


END onetime_pkg;
/
Output Package body created
```

```
--Checking the procedure

BEGIN
   IF onetime_pkg.sal_greater_maxsal (9000)
   THEN
      DBMS_OUTPUT.put_line ('Salary is greated the maximum salary');
   ELSE
      DBMS_OUTPUT.put_line ('Salary is less the maximum salary');
   END IF;
END;
/
Output
Salary is greated the maximum salary
PL/SQL procedure successfully completed.
```

Declare PL/SQL composite data types in a package

PL/SQL composite data types can be declared in the packages as an alternative to create at data base level.

The following example creates a package with one PL/SQL table and one procedure, the procedure have a parameter of OUT mode of PL/SQL table type, the package body selects the entire data of EMP table and assigns to the parameter and at last there is a PL/SQL program to call the packaged procedure because procedure returns table type so a variable of the similar table type is declared to accept the data.
NOTE: The package's parameter can be only of table type when the table type is declared in the package or database.

Example 1

```
--Creation of Package specification
-- With one table type and one procedure
-- The parameter of procedure is of emp_ty type
CREATE OR REPLACE PACKAGE emp_table_pkg
IS
   TYPE emp_ty IS TABLE OF emp%ROWTYPE
      INDEX BY BINARY_INTEGER;

   PROCEDURE my_proc (p_emp OUT emp_ty);
END;
/

--Creation of package body
--Cursor is declared to select all data of emp table
--The data is assigned to p_emp parameter to take out
CREATE OR REPLACE PACKAGE BODY emp_table_pkg
IS
   PROCEDURE my_proc (p_emp OUT emp_ty)
   IS
      CURSOR v_cur
```

```
        IS
            SELECT *
            FROM    emp;

        i    NUMBER := 1;
    BEGIN
        OPEN v_cur;

        LOOP
            EXIT WHEN v_cur%NOTFOUND;

            FETCH v_cur
            INTO  p_emp (i);

            i     := i + 1;
        END LOOP;
    END;
END;
/


--Program to test the package
--v_emp is of emp_table_pkg.emp_ty type
DECLARE
    v_emp    emp_table_pkg.emp_ty;
BEGIN
    emp_table_pkg.my_proc (v_emp);

    FOR i IN v_emp.FIRST .. v_emp.LAST


    LOOP
        DBMS_OUTPUT.put_line (    'EMPNO='
                                || v_emp (i).empno
                                || '   ENAME='
                                || v_emp (i).ename
                                || '   SAL='
                                || v_emp (i).sal
                            );
    END LOOP;
END;
/


Output
EMPNO=7369   ENAME=SMITHXDCF   SAL=880.11
EMPNO=7499   ENAME=ALLEN    SAL=1600
EMPNO=7521   ENAME=WARD    SAL=1250
EMPNO=7566   ENAME=JONES    SAL=2975
EMPNO=7654   ENAME=MARTIN    SAL=1250
EMPNO=7698   ENAME=BLAKE    SAL=2850
EMPNO=7782   ENAME=CLARK    SAL=2450
EMPNO=7788   ENAME=SCOTT    SAL=3000
EMPNO=7839   ENAME=KING    SAL=5000
EMPNO=7844   ENAME=TURNER    SAL=1500
EMPNO=7876   ENAME=ADAMS    SAL=1100
EMPNO=7900   ENAME=JAMES    SAL=17600
EMPNO=7902   ENAME=Farhan    SAL=3000


PL/SQL procedure successfully completed.
```

Restrictions on packaged functions used in SQL

A packaged function that is called in SQL SELECT statements or DML statements cannot contain COMMIT, ROLLBACK, SAVE POINT and ALTER SYSTEM or ALTER SESSION statements. A packaged function that is called in the DML statements cannot contain DML statements or SELECT statements that alter or query the same table that DML statement is altering , table is mutating error will raise otherwise.

Example

```
CREATE OR REPLACE PACKAGE restrict_pkg
IS
   FUNCTION upd_table (p_emp NUMBER)
      RETURN NUMBER;
END;
/
Output
Package created


CREATE OR REPLACE PACKAGE BODY restrict_pkg
IS
   FUNCTION upd_table (p_emp NUMBER)
      RETURN NUMBER
   IS
      v_sal    NUMBER;
   BEGIN
      SELECT sal
      INTO   v_sal
      FROM   emp
      WHERE  empno = p_emp;

      IF v_sal > 1000
      THEN
         RETURN 200;
      ELSE
         RETURN 100;
      END IF;
   END;
END restrict_pkg;
/
Output
Package body created
```

```
UPDATE emp
SET sal = restrict_pkg.upd_table (7900)
WHERE  empno = 7900;
/
```

Output
SET sal = restrict_pkg.upd_table (7900)
     *

ERROR at line 2:
ORA-04091: table SCOTT.EMP is mutating, trigger/function may not see it
ORA-06512: at "SCOTT.RESTRICT_PKG", line 8

Summary

In this chapter you have learned that packages improve management, security, organization and performance, logically related data is combined in one container.
You can change package body without effecting package specification, When package is first invoked it is loaded in user's memory so further calls reduce network traffic.
Overloading can be done to the packaged procedures or functions, forward referencing can be done in the packages which allow to call a subprogram before writing it, A onetime only procedure executes once when the package is first invoked within user's schema and PL/SQL composite data types can be declared in the packages as an alternative to declaring at database level.

Exercise

1. Create a package with one public procedure and a private function , The procedure should increment the salary of the employees having salary less then 8000, Use the private function to decide that whether the employee is eligible of an increment or not.

2 . Create an overloaded procedure, first procedure should accept one parameter of EMPNO and raise the employee's salary by 10%, and second procedure should accept one parameter of EMPNO and one parameter of increment percent and raise the employee's salary accordingly.

3 . What is wrong with the following example

```
CREATE OR REPLACE PACKAGE comm_pkg
IS
--Procedure will give 10% commission
-- to the employee who has sal less then 8000
```

```
PROCEDURE emp_com (p_empno NUMBER);
END;
/

----------------------
----------------------
--package body

CREATE OR REPLACE PACKAGE BODY comm_pkg
IS
   PROCEDURE emp_com (p_empno NUMBER)
   IS
   BEGIN
      --If the employee is elgible give him commission
      IF emp_com_elgible (p_empno)
      THEN
         UPDATE emp
         SET comm = sal * .10
         WHERE  empno = p_empno;

         COMMIT;
      ELSE
         raise_application_error (-20050, 'Not elgible of commission');
      END IF;
   END;
----------------------
   --Privat function
--Function will return True, if the employee's
--salary is less then 8000
   FUNCTION emp_com_elgible (p_empno NUMBER)
      RETURN BOOLEAN
   IS
      v_sal   NUMBER (10);
   BEGIN
      SELECT sal
      INTO   v_sal
      FROM   emp
      WHERE  empno = p_empno;

      IF v_sal > 8000
      THEN
         RETURN FALSE;
      ELSE
         RETURN TRUE;
      END IF;
   EXCEPTION
      WHEN NO_DATA_FOUND
      THEN
         RETURN FALSE;
   END;
END;
/
```

4.   Give an example of forwarding referring.

5. Create a package with onetime only procedure, the onetime only procedure should get the salary of any particular employee into a packaged variable, print the variable value, then update that employee's salary and print the variable value, the value should not be changed as onetime only procedure executes only once in a schema.

6. The following is a schema of one time only procedure, is it correct, if not then what should be done to correct it.

```
CREATE OR REPLACE PACKAGE BODY package_name
IS
--variables
--cursors
--programe units

--One time only procedure
BEGIN
--Statement 1
--Statement 2
END;
END;
```

7. When following packaged procedure is called it raises an error that "too many declarations of 'OVERLOAD_PROC' match this call", what's the problem?

```
Create or replace package overload_num_pkg
 is
 procedure overload_proc(p_number NUMBER);
 procedure overload_proc(p_number INTEGER);
 end;
/
 Create or replace package body overload_num_pkg
 is
 procedure overload_proc(p_number NUMBER)
 is
 BEGIN
 dbms_output.put_line(p_number);
 end;
 procedure overload_proc(p_number INTEGER)
 is
 BEGIN
 dbms_output.put_line(p_number);
 end; end;
```

16 TRIGGERS

In this chapter you will learn this

What is a trigger?
Benefits of using a trigger
Trigger event
Trigger type
Trigger code
Trigger creation
Statement and row level triggers
Instead of triggers
Compound triggers

We have covered anonyms PL/SQL blocks and named Program units (Procedures, functions and packages), in this chapter we will cover another type of named PL/SQL block called trigger.

What is a trigger?

A trigger is a named PL/SQL block that performs some action on a particular event.
For example you are inserting a record into employee's table and you want that after inserting the record into employee's table the same record should be inserted into employee_beckup table, you can achieve this by using a trigger.
It means inserting the record into the employee's table is an event and an action is required to insert the same record into employee_backup table, after that event the action is performed by trigger.
An event causes a trigger to fire; means causes a trigger to execute.

Benefits of using a Trigger

1. Provide security
2. Implementing complex business rules
3. Restrict invalid data
4. Providing value auditing

Trigger Event

The trigger event can be any as following

1. A DML statement as Insert, Update, Delete. The trigger is associated with the
    Table and can fire for any Insert, Update, Delete. For example you are going to update any
    particular row of any table and at that table there is a trigger which execute before updating
    any row to check that the day is not a holiday.
    Trigger event is specified into trigger header.

2. A DDL statement (Create, Alter, Drop). Trigger can be written for any particular user or for
    all users of a schema, these kinds of triggers are particularly useful for DBAs to maintain
    history of the modifications applied to the database objects.

3. A system event such as startup or shutdown of the database.

4. A user event, for example logging on and off. These triggers are useful if you want to
    maintain history of a particular user or all users' logging on and off.

    In this book we will cover only triggers which are fired by DML statements.

Trigger Type

The trigger type defines that, when the trigger will fire in response to the triggering event? , For
example trigger should fire before an insertion into a table or trigger should fire after an insertion into
a table?
Trigger type is specified into trigger header as 'before insert into employee'.

Trigger code

Trigger code is written similarly as of standard PL/SQL block, the difference is only in header
section.

Trigger creation

Syntax

```
 CREATE [OR REPLACE] TRIGGER trigger_name
  {Before|After} Triggering_event on table_name
[for each row]
[follows an other trigger]
[ENABLE|DISABLE]
[WHEN clause]
DECLARE
………
BEGIN
…………
…………
EXCEPTION
…………
…………..
END;
```

The keyword CREATE is used to indicate that some object is going to generate, OR REPLACE is used to drop the object if the object already exists, TRIGGER key word confirms that it is trigger which is going to generate.
BEFORE|AFTER shows that either the trigger will execute before the triggering statement or after triggering statement, TRIGGERING EVENT is the statement which causes the trigger to fire (For example INSERT, UPDATE, DELETE). TABLE_NAME is the table associated.
[for each row] indicates that the trigger is row level trigger, explained later in this chapter.
[Follows another trigger] and [ENABLE|DISABLE] are oracle 11g features.
[Follows another trigger] allows the order in which triggers at the same level will fire,
Previously oracle did not guarantee that if two "after insert" triggers are at the same table then which will fire first.
[Follows another trigger] is used to specify that after which trigger this trigger will fire.
The trigger specified in this clause should be at the same level, means if you are creating after insert trigger at department table then trigger in follows clause should also be of type "after insert" at department table.
Prior to oracle 11g ALTER statement was used to ENABLE|DISABLE a trigger, Trigger was always in ENABLE state when it was created.
Now you can specify the ENABLE|DISABLE state at creation time, a DISABLED trigger will not fire.
If ENABLE|DISABLE is not specified then the trigger will be ENABLED by default.

In [When clause] a condition can be specified, which should meet to execute the trigger code (can be used only with row level triggers).
OLD and NEW qualifiers are used to refer old and new values of columns (can be used only with row level triggers).
All other section is same as that of PL/SQL block.

Statement and row level triggers

Statement level triggers execute once for each triggering statement, no matter how many rows are affected by the triggering statement or no row is affected at all.
For example you write a trigger to insert a record in a table X whenever a user executes update statement against employee's table, the trigger will insert one record into the table X even if the update statement has not affected one record or it has affected 100 records.
Row level triggers execute as many times as the number of rows affected.
For example you write a trigger on employee table to record the changes in table X that has been done by any user, so when the user will update the rows in employees table the trigger will execute as many time as the number of rows affected and inserts the record to other table one by one and if the triggering statement will not update any row the trigger will not execute.

Statement level triggers

In the following example a statement level trigger is created at emp table, after executing update statement at emp the trigger emp_update_info will insert information into emp_upd_info table the date On which the updating is done and the user who have done the updating.

Example 1

For this example first create a table as following

```
CREATE   TABLE emp_upd_info(date_upd DATE,user_upd VARCHAR2(30))
/
```

After that execute the following statement to create trigger

```
CREATE OR REPLACE TRIGGER emp_update_info
   AFTER UPDATE
   ON emp
BEGIN
--contains date of updation and the user name who updated
   INSERT INTO emp_upd_info
               (date_upd,
                user_upd
               )
   VALUES      (SYSDATE,
                USER
               );
END;
/
Output
Trigger created
```

To test the trigger, run the following update command

```
UPDATE emp
SET sal = 4000
WHERE  empno = 7900
/
Output
One row updated
```

Now query the emp_upd_info table to check that the trigger worked or not as following

```
SELECT *
FROM   emp_upd_info
/
```

```
Output
DATE_UPD   USER_UPD
```

```
--------- ---------
21-MAY-09 SCOTT
```

 Run update statement with different EMPNO and check that emp_upd_info table populated with value, you will note that the trigger will execute even if no record is updated in the EMP table. The above trigger is used to insert one record into emp_upd_info table whenever an updating is performed on emp table to track the user who have performed DML, you can also specify two events in one trigger, for example you want to do the same functionality but after update of emp table or after insert into emp table as following

Example 2

```
CREATE OR REPLACE TRIGGER emp_update_info
    AFTER UPDATE OR INSERT
    ON emp
BEGIN
--contains date of updation and the user name who updated
    INSERT INTO emp_upd_info
                (date_upd,
                 user_upd
                )
    VALUES      (SYSDATE,
                 USER
                );
END;
/
```

To test insert one row into emp table as

```
INSERT INTO emp
              (empno,
               ename,
               job,
               mgr,
               hiredate,
               sal,
               comm,
               deptno,
               age
               )
    (SELECT 1122,
            'FARHAN',
            job,
            mgr,
            hiredate,
            15000,
            comm,
            deptno,
            age
    FROM    emp
    WHERE   empno = 7900)
/
```

Now query the emp_upd_info table to check that the trigger worked or not as following

```
SELECT *
FROM    emp_upd_info
/
Output
DATE_UPD   USER_UPD
--------- ---------
21-MAY-09 SCOTT
```

The same trigger will perform same action after insert or after update.

Note: that after each example, I rollback the changes that's why only one row is shown in above example.

You can specify any particular DML operation by using keywords INSERTING, UPDATING or
DELETING inside an if statement as following

Example 3

```
CREATE OR REPLACE TRIGGER emp_update_info
    AFTER UPDATE OR INSERT
    ON emp
BEGIN
--contains date of updation or insertion and the user name
    IF INSERTING
    THEN
        INSERT INTO emp_upd_info
                    (date_upd,
                     user_upd
                    )
        VALUES      (SYSDATE,
                     USER || ' Insertion'
                    );
    ELSIF UPDATING
    THEN
        INSERT INTO emp_upd_info
                    (date_upd,
                     user_upd
                    )
        VALUES      (SYSDATE,
                     USER || ' Updation'
                    );
    END IF;
END;
/
```

This means you can perform different actions on different DML operations.

In the above example the trigger fired after an update is performed on emp table, you can also specify
one specific column say C for which the trigger will fire, if the an update is performed on any other
column than C the trigger will not fire, the column can be specified only for the update statement.
The following example is used to perform some action when the Sal column of the EMP table is
updated

Example 4

```
CREATE OR REPLACE TRIGGER emp_update_info
    AFTER UPDATE OF sal
    ON emp
BEGIN
```

```
--contains date of updation and the user name who updated
    INSERT INTO emp_upd_info
                (date_upd,
                 user_upd
                )
    VALUES      (SYSDATE,
                 USER
                );
END;
/
Output
Trigger created
```

To test the trigger, run the following update command

```
UPDATE emp
SET sal = 4000
WHERE   empno = 7900
/
Output
One row updated
```

Now query the emp_upd_info table to check that the trigger worked or not as following

```
SELECT *
FROM    emp_upd_info
/
Output
DATE_UPD   USER_UPD
---------  ---------
21-MAY-09  SCOTT
```

One row inserted into emp_upd_info table because Sal column of the Emp table is updated, Now check by updating any other column of the emp table as

```
UPDATE emp
SET ename = 'FARHAN'
WHERE   empno = 7900
/
Output
One row updated
```

Now query the emp_upd_info table to check that the trigger worked or not as following

```
SELECT *
FROM    emp_upd_info
/
Output
DATE_UPD   USER_UPD
---------  ---------
```

Note: that no row is updated because the updated column is not SAL.

You can also specify more than one column in the trigger as in the following example; the following trigger will fire when the "SAL" or "ENAME" column is updated.

Example 5

```
CREATE OR REPLACE TRIGGER emp_update_info
    AFTER UPDATE OF sal,ename
    ON emp
BEGIN
--contains date of updation and the user name who updated
    INSERT INTO emp_upd_info
                (date_upd,
                 user_upd
                )
    VALUES      (SYSDATE,
                 USER
                );
END;
/
Output
Trigger created
```

To test the trigger, run the following update command

```
UPDATE emp
SET ENAME ='FARHAN'
WHERE   empno = 7900
/
Output
One row updated
```

Now query the emp_upd_info table to check that the trigger worked or not as following

```
SELECT *
FROM    emp_upd_info
/
Output
DATE_UPD   USER_UPD
--------- ---------
21-MAY-09 SCOTT
```

Row level triggers

Row level triggers fire for each row effect by the triggering statement.
In the following example a row level trigger is created which will execute after an update of each row and insert its old values in the emp_test table for maintaining history.
Create emp_test with same structure as of emp table.

Example 1

```
CREATE OR REPLACE TRIGGER emp_update_history
    AFTER UPDATE
    ON emp
    FOR EACH ROW
BEGIN
-- :old is a qualifier used to refer the old value of the column        --
explained later
    INSERT INTO emp_test
                (empno,
                 ename,
                 job,
                 mgr,
                 hiredate,
                 sal,
                 comm,
                 deptno,
                 age
                )
    VALUES      (:OLD.empno,
                 :OLD.ename,
                 :OLD.job,
                 :OLD.mgr,
                 :OLD.hiredate,
                 :OLD.sal,
                 :OLD.comm,
                 :OLD.deptno,
                 :OLD.age
                );
END;
/
Output
Trigger created
```

To test the trigger execute the following statement

```
UPDATE emp
SET sal = 8000
WHERE   sal < 8000 AND sal > 500
/
Output
12 rows updated
```

Note: that the 12 rows are update and 12 rows should be inserted into emp_test table for maintaining history, query emp_test table as

```
SELECT empno,
       ename,
       sal
FROM   emp_test
/
```

Output

EMPNO	ENAME	SAL
9866	farhan	1000
A455	abcdef	2000
7566	FAISAL	2000
7654	MARTIN	2000
7698	BLAKE	2000
7782	SHAHZAD	2000
7788	SCOTT	2000
7839	KINGS	2000
7844	TURNER	2000
7876	ADAMS	2000
7900	JAMES	2000

EMPNO	ENAME	SAL
7902	FORD	2000

12 rows selected

Try to update row for nonexistent employee, you will note that trigger will not fire even once unlike Statement level triggers.
"When clause" is used to specify the condition that should meet for the trigger to execute.

Example 2

```
CREATE OR REPLACE TRIGGER emp_update_history
    AFTER UPDATE
    ON emp
    FOR EACH ROW
    WHEN (OLD.ENAME='FARHAN')
BEGIN
-- :old is a qualifier used to refer the old value of the column        --
explained later
    INSERT INTO emp_test
                (empno,
                 ename,
                 job,
                 mgr,
                 hiredate,
                 sal,
                 comm,
                 deptno,
                 age
                )
    VALUES      (:OLD.empno,
                 :OLD.ename,
                 :OLD.job,
                 :OLD.mgr,
                 :OLD.hiredate,
                 :OLD.sal,
                 :OLD.comm,
                 :OLD.deptno,
                 :OLD.age
                );
END;
/
Output
Trigger created
```

Execute the following statement to test

```
UPDATE emp
SET sal = 1000;
/
Output
13 rows updated
```

Now query the emp_test table, note that only one record is inserted into emp_test table because trigger executed only for the record where ename is equal to "FARHAN".

```
SELECT empno,
       ename,
       sal
FROM   emp_test
/
```

Output

EMPNO	ENAME	SAL
1122	FARHAN	15000

Note that OLD is not prefixed with the colons in header, because the OLD and NEW qualifiers do not require a colon prefix when they are referred outside the trigger body.

Instead of triggers

Instead of triggers are defined on complex views, complex views are not modified by normal DML operations.
As you know that on simple views insertion, updating or deletion can be preformed but on complex view DML operations are achieved by Instead of triggers.
When instead of trigger is defined on a view than the trigger executes in place of triggering statement, triggering statement is not executed at all.

Creation of instead of triggers

Syntax

CREATE [OR REPLACE] TRIGGER trigger_name
 INSTEAD OF Triggering_event on view_name
 For each row
DECLARE
....
BEGIN
....
....
EXCEPTION
....
....
END;

CREATE [OR REPLACE] TRIGGER indicates that a trigger is going to generate, trigger_name is the name of the trigger, INSTEAD OF indicates the type of trigger, Triggering_event can be any DML statement (INSERT, UPDATE, DELETE), ON view_name is the name of the view (Simple) on which the trigger is going to generate, For each row indicates that INSTEAD OF TRIGGER is defined at row level (INSTEAD OF TRIGGER can only be of row level type), All other block sections are similar as that of PL/SQL block;

Note: An instead of trigger can only be defined at row level.

The following example creates a complex view and deletes one row from the view; row cannot be deleted so the following error is raised

Example 1

```
-- A complex view creation
CREATE OR REPLACE VIEW dept_emp_vw
AS
    SELECT     e.deptno,
               d.dname,
               COUNT (empno) emps
    FROM       emp e, dept d
    WHERE      e.deptno = d.deptno
    GROUP BY e.deptno, d.dname
/
Output
Trigger created


--Delete from the view
DELETE FROM dept_emp_vw
WHERE          deptno = 10
/
Output
delete from dept_emp_vw where deptno=10
               *
ERROR at line 1:
ORA-01732: data manipulation operation not legal on this view
```

This error can be avoided and deletion can be performed on view by creating following trigger, in the following trigger the row is deleted from the EMP table on which the view is based, Instead of trigger will fire in place of delete statement and one row will be deleted from EMP table.

Example 2

```
--Instead of trigger generated
CREATE OR REPLACE TRIGGER dept_emp_trig
    INSTEAD OF DELETE
    ON dept_emp_vw
    FOR EACH ROW
BEGIN
    DELETE FROM emp
    WHERE          deptno = :OLD.deptno;
END;
/

--Delete from the view
DELETE FROM dept_emp_vw
WHERE          deptno = 10
/
Output
1 row deleted
```

Compound Triggers

A compound trigger can have all trigger types, BEFOR and AFTER Statement, BEFORE and AFTER row level triggers in one trigger.

The compound trigger makes it easier to program an approach where you want the actions you implement for the various timing points to share common data. To achieve the same effect with simple triggers, you had to model the common state with an ancillary package. This approach was both difficult to program and subject to memory leak when the triggering statement caused an error and the after-statement trigger did not fire.

A compound trigger has an optional declarative part and a section for each of its timing points. All of these sections can access a common PL/SQL state. The common state is established when the triggering statement starts and is destroys when the triggering statement completes, even when the triggering statement causes an error.

Syntax
CREATE [OR REPLACE] TRIGGER trigger_name
Triggering_event ON table_name
COMPOUND TRIGGER

Declaration section

BEFORE STATEMENT IS
BEGIN
STATEMETN1;
STATEMENT2;
………………..
EXCEPTION
STATEMENT1;

………………..
END BEFORE STATEMETN;

BEFORE EACH ROW IS
BEGIN
STATEMETN1;
STATEMENT2;

………………..
EXCEPTION
STATEMENT1;
………………..
END BEFORE EACH ROW;

AFTER EACH ROW IS
BEGIN
STATEMETN1;
STATEMENT2;
………………..
EXCEPTION
STATEMENT1;
………………..
END AFTER EACH ROW;

AFTER STATEMENT IS
BEGIN
STATEMETN1;
STATEMENT2;
………………..
EXCEPTION
STATEMENT1;
………………..
END AFTER STATEMETN;

END;

Note the BEFOR and AFTER keywords are not used in the Header.

In the following example compound trigger is generated for emp_upd_info and emp_upd_history tables which were created in the row level and statement level trigger, drop both triggers and create this to get the functionality of both triggers as

Example 1

```
CREATE OR REPLACE TRIGGER COMP_TRIGG
FOR UPDATE ON EMP
COMPOUND TRIGGER
AFTER STATEMENT IS
BEGIN
INSERT INTO emp_upd_info
                (date_upd,
                 user_upd
                )
    VALUES      (SYSDATE,
                 USER
                );
END;
AFTER EACH ROW IS
BEGIN
    INSERT INTO emp_test
                (empno,
                 ename,
                 job,
                 mgr,
                 hiredate,
                 sal,
                 comm,
                 deptno,
                 age
                )
    VALUES      (:OLD.empno,
                 :OLD.ename,
                 :OLD.job,
                 :OLD.mgr,
                 :OLD.hiredate,
                 :OLD.sal,
                 :OLD.comm,
                 :OLD.deptno,
                 :OLD.age
                );
END;
END
/

Output
Trigger created
```

To test the trigger execute the following statement

```
UPDATE emp
SET sal = 8000
WHERE   sal < 8000 AND sal > 500
/
Output
12 rows updated
```

Note that 12 rows are updated but only one row should be inserted into emp_upd_info as a result of trigger fire, because statement trigger is used to insert the row, query the emp_upd_info table as

```
SELECT *
FROM    emp_upd_info
/
Output
DATE_UPD   USER_UPD
---------- ----------
21-MAY-09  SCOTT
```

12 rows are update so 12 rows should be inserted into emp_test table for maintaining history. "After each row" is used inside the trigger body to insert rows into emp_test.

```
SELECT empno,
       ename,
       sal
FROM   emp_test
/
```

Output

EMPNO	ENAME	SAL
9866	farhan	1000
A455	abcdef	2000
7566	FAISAL	2000
7654	MARTIN	2000
7698	BLAKE	2000
7782	SHAHZAD	2000
7788	SCOTT	2000
7839	KINGS	2000
7844	TURNER	2000
7876	ADAMS	2000
7900	JAMES	2000

EMPNO	ENAME	SAL
7902	FORD	2000

12 rows selected

Restrictions on compound trigger

1. A compound trigger can be defined on the DML statements of the Table or View only.
2. A compound trigger cannot have antonymous transactions, which mean that the Declarative part cannot include PRAGMA AUTONOMOUS_TRANSACTION
3. EXCEPTION occurred in one executable section doesn't propagate in the other section so exception should be handled within the section for example exception occurred in after each row should be handled in that section.
4. Like before the OLD and NEW qualifiers cannot be used in BEFOR STATEMENT and AFTER STATEMENT sections and in compound triggers one more restriction is that you cannot use OLD and NEW qualifiers in Declaration section as well.
5. If a section includes a GOTO statement, the target of the GOTO statement must be in the same section.
6. If compound triggers are ordered using the FOLLOWS option, and if the target of FOLLOWS does not contain the corresponding section as source code, the ordering is ignored

Note
(Autonomous transactions allow you to leave the context of the calling transaction, perform an independent transaction, and return to the calling transaction without affecting its state. The autonomous transaction has no link to the calling transaction, so only committed data can be shared by both transactions.).

Summary

In this chapter you have learned that trigger is a PL/SQL block which executes on some specific event, the event can be any DML, DDL, DCL or System action but in this chapter you have learned about triggers executed on DML events.
Statement level trigger executes once even if no rows is affected at all but row level trigger executes the number of times the rows are affected by triggering event.
OLD and NEW qualifiers are used with row level triggers only.
Instead of trigger executes in place of triggering statement causing DML operations against a view, Instead of trigger can be defined at row level only.
Compound trigger is defined to contain all the statement and row triggers of a table.

Exercise

1. Create a table of same structure as of EMP table, and write a trigger that should insert the deleted record of EMP table into that new table.

2. Create a new table emp_dml_info with columns c_date and c_user, write a trigger that should insert date and user name on each dml operation.
   Keep the type of c_user varchar2 with 50 as length.

3. Change the above trigger so that is should not only get the user name into user column but it should also name the DML operation performed as following
   SCOTT, UPDATION HAS BEEN PERFORMED
   SCOTT, DELETION HAS BEEN PERFORMED
   SCOTT, INSERTION HAS BEEN PERFORMED

4. What is wrong with the following statement

```
CREATE OR REPLACE TRIGGER COMP_TRIGG
FOR UPDATE ON EMP
AFTER STATEMENT IS
BEGIN
INSERT INTO emp_upd_info
              (date_upd,
               user_upd
              )
    VALUES    (SYSDATE,
               USER
```

```
                    );
END;
END
/
```

5. Create a view with following code and define an instead of trigger against this view to perform DML operations

```
--Simple view
CREATE OR REPLACE VIEW emp_vw
AS
    SELECT  empno,
            ename
    FROM    emp
/
```

17 USING ORACLE OBJECT TYPES

In this chapter you will learn about

Introduction to oracle objects
Declaring and initializing objects
Declaring and manipulating Objects in PL/SQL
Defining object methods
Declaring and using nested tables
Declaring and using VARRAYs

Introduction

Object-oriented programming consists on reusable components and complex applications. In PL/SQL object-oriented programming is based on object types. They let you model real-world objects, separate interfaces and implementation details, and store object-oriented data presently in the database.

Oracle objects

An object type is a user defined composite data type representing a data structure   and functions and procedures to manipulate the data.
The variables within the data structure are called attributes, the functions and procedures are called methods.
An object type has attributes and actions.

For example, a human has the attributes gender, age, and weight, height and the actions eat, work, and sleep. Object type let you represent such real-world behavior in the application.

Why use object types?

A large system can be broken into logical entities by using object types.
This lets you create software components that are modular, maintainable and reusable across platforms and teams. Object types and their methods are stored in the database, so they are available for any application to use.
Developer can benefit from the work that is already done and no need to re-create similar structures in every application.
You can fetch and manipulate a set of related objects as a single unit. A single request to fetch the object from server can fetch other related objects by object references.

Declaring and initializing objects

Syntax

CREATE [OR REPLACE] TYPE type name AS OBJECT
  Attribute name data type,
  MEMBER PROCEDURE | FUNCTION procedure or function spec, …….
  [MAP | ORDER MEMBER FUNCTION <comparison function spec>, ...]
  [PRAGMA RESTRICT_REFERENCES (<what to restrict>, restrictions)]
   );

CREATE keyword indicates that a data base object is going to generate, [OR REPLACE] keyword is used to delete the object if it already exists, TYPE keyword indicates that it is Type which is going to generate, type_name is the name of type, AS OBJECT indicates that it is an Object which is going to generate.
Attributes will contain elements, attributes can be one or more, attributes are like columns of a table so each attribute's data type is specified.
MEMBER PROCEDURE | FUNCTION is used to declare a procedure or function called Method.

Example 1

The following code creates an object type for storing addresses
Of employees, creates a table and manipulates the table.

```
CREATE OR REPLACE TYPE sample_add_type AS OBJECT (
        Street    VARCHAR2 (50),
        City      VARCHAR2 (30)
            );
            /
        Output
        Type Created
```

The following statement creates a table with column address of type sample_add_type object type
which has street and city, sample_table have both street and city as columns by referring the
object type instead of declaring the columns separately.

```
CREATE TABLE sample_table
        (Employee_id NUMBER,
         Name VARCHAR2 (30),
         Address sample_add_type)
         /
        Output
        Table created
```

Date can be inserted into sample_table as following, in values clause the values are inserted into
address column by referring the object type and by giving the value of its each attribute inside
brackets.

```
INSERT INTO sample_table
VALUES       (100,
              'ALI',
              sample_add_type ('501 STREET', 'KARACHI')
              )
              /
          Output
          1 row created
```

In Select statement the column values of address are referred by using column name followed by each attribute's name as

```
SELECT  e.employee_id ID,
        e.address.city city,
        e.address.street str
FROM    sample_table e
/
Output
```

ID CITY   STR

---------- --

100 KARACHI   501 STREETSTR

Similarly in update Statement

```
UPDATE sample_table e
   SET e.address.city = 'NEW YORK'
WHERE  employee_id = 100
/
Output
1 row updated
```

Declaring and manipulating object in PL/SQL

After an object type is defined and installed in the schema, you can use it to declare objects in any PL/SQL block, subprogram, or package.

For example, you can use the object type to specify the data type of an attribute, column, variable, bind variable, record field, table element, formal parameter, or function result.

At run time, instances of the object type are created that is, objects of that type are instantiated. Each object can hold different values.

The following code declares a variable of object type and does some manipulation.

Example 1

```
DECLARE
v_emp      sample_add_type;
BEGIN
    v_emp      := sample_add_type ('701 street', 'Karachi');
DBMS_OUTPUT.put_line (v_emp.street || ' ' || v_emp.city);
END;
 /
```

```
Output
```
701 street Karachi
PL/SQL procedure successfully completed.

Defining object methods

Like packaged subprograms, methods have two parts, a specification and a body.
The specification consists of a method name and an optional parameter List and   for functions a return type.
The body is the code that executes to perform specific tasks.
 If PL/SQL type doesn't declare any Method then only Specification is required, Otherwise body is also required.

Methods can be written in PL/SQL, Java and C.
Methods are declared by using the keyword MEMBER or STATIC.
MEMBER methods are invoked on instances as

```
Instance_Expression.method();
```

STATIC methods are invoked on the object type not on instances

```
Object_Type.method();
```

The following code shows the use of MEMBER methods

The following statement creates and objects as

```
CREATE TYPE add_type AS OBJECT (
                street    VARCHAR2 (50),
                city      VARCHAR2 (20)
                );
                /
                Output
                Type Created
```

The following statement creates another object referring the above object and declaring MEMBER function and procedure.

Example 1

```
CREATE OR REPLACE TYPE emp_type AS OBJECT (
 Employee_id    NUMBER (6),
 NAME           VARCHAR2 (30),
 Address        add_type,
 MAP MEMBER FUNCTION ID
   RETURN NUMBER,
 MEMBER PROCEDURE display_address (SELF IN OUT emp_type)
 )
 /
Output
Type created
```

Note: SELF is a parameter that contains the instance of the object type, it should always be the first parameter in procedure or function, and if this parameter is not given as in the above function ID the parameter is automatically declared.

The following statement creates type body to implement Methods similarly as in   Packages

```
CREATE OR REPLACE TYPE BODY emp_type
AS
 MAP MEMBER FUNCTION ID
     RETURN NUMBER
 IS
 BEGIN
     RETURN (employee_id);
 END;
 MEMBER PROCEDURE display_address (SELF IN OUT NOCOPY emp_type)
 IS
 BEGIN
     DBMS_OUTPUT.put_line (NAME || ' ' || address.street || ' '
                           || address.city
                          );
 END;
 END
 /

 Output
 Type body created
```

The following statement is used to create the table of the type emp_type.

```
CREATE TABLE emp_table OF emp_type
/

Output
Table created
```

The following statement is used to insert a record into emp_table table.

```
 INSERT INTO emp_table
          (employee_id,
           NAME,
           address
          )
  VALUES      (100,
           'Ali',
           add_type ('701 street', 'karachi')
          )
/

Output
1 row created
```

The following example shows the use of MEMBER procedure Display_address, The member function is called on instance, the procedure is called here on EMP instance.

```
DECLARE
   emp     emp_type;
BEGIN
   emp       := emp_type (10, 'ALI', add_type ('781 MISSION', 'KARACHI'));
   emp.display_address ();
   END
   /

   Output
```
ALI 781 MISSION KARACHI
PL/SQL procedure successfully completed.

Note that the procedure displays the values which are passed in the same block because MEMBER procedures are called on the instance.

The following code shows the use of STATIC methods

Example 2

```
CREATE OR REPLACE TYPE st_type AS OBJECT (
   v_var    NUMBER,
   STATIC PROCEDURE ID (p_number NUMBER)
);
   /

Output
Type created
```

The type body simply implements the ID procedure; the procedure takes the number and prints it.

```
CREATE OR REPLACE TYPE BODY st_type
AS
   STATIC PROCEDURE ID (p_number NUMBER)
   IS
   BEGIN
     NULL;
     DBMS_OUTPUT.put_line (p_number);
   END;
END;
   /

Output
Type body created
```

These Methods are called similarly as packaged subprograms. The method's name is prefixed by the type name as

```
EXEC st_type.id (12);

Output
12
PL/SQL procedure successfully completed
```

Collection Types

To store nested tables and varies inside database tables, you must also declare SQL types using the create statement. The SQL types can be used as columns or as attributes of SQL object types. An object can have other objects as attributes, and the attribute Objects can have object attributes too. An entire part-list hierarchy can be built up in this way from interlocking object types.

The following code shows the use of nested object types

Nested tables

Nested table types can also be generated at database levels.
The advantage of declaring the nested table types at data base level is that the variables of nested table that are declared in the PL/SQL block can be used in SQL statements.
All the other procedure of using nested table is same as that of nested tables declared at the block level.

Syntax

CREATE TYPE type_name IS TABLE OF datatype||object type;

CREATE TYPE indicates that it is type that is going to generate, type_name is the name of the type, IS TABLE OF indicates that it is nested table that is going to generate, data type is used to give a data type if the nested table contains only one column and if nested table contains more than one column then object type is first created.

The following statement creates a table type as

Example 1

```
CREATE TYPE dnames_tab AS TABLE OF VARCHAR2 (30)
    /
Output
Type created
```

The following statement creates a table depts with one column dept_names based on table type
dnames_tab.

```
CREATE TABLE depts (region VARCHAR2(25),
                                    dept_names dnames_tab)
    NESTED TABLE dept_names STORE AS dnames_nt;
  Output
  Table Created
```

The following block is used to insert three rows in depts table , against each row there are many
values in the dept_names table, For example in the row where region is equal to 'Europe'
dept_names have three values as 'Shipping','Sales','Finance',
It is similar if you make a parent table which contain one regain row and a child table containing
multiple dept_names again one parent region.

```
BEGIN
   INSERT INTO depts
   VALUES         ('Europe',
                   dnames_tab ('Shipping', 'Sales', 'Finance')
                   );

   INSERT INTO depts
   VALUES         ('Americas',
                   dnames_tab ('Sales', 'Finance', 'Shipping')
                   );

   INSERT INTO depts
   VALUES         ('Asia',
                   dnames_tab ('Finance', 'Payroll')
                   );

   COMMIT;
   END;
   /

   Output
   PL/SQL procedure successfully completed
```

In the following example it is shown that how we can get the values of a nested table within a table.

```
DECLARE
    v_dnames    dnames_tab;
BEGIN
    SELECT  dept_names
    INTO    v_dnames
    FROM    depts
    WHERE   region = 'Europe';

    FOR i IN v_dnames.FIRST .. v_dnames.LAST
    LOOP
        DBMS_OUTPUT.put_line (v_dnames (i));
    END LOOP;
END;
    /

Output
Shipping
Sales
Finance
PL/SQL procedure successfully completed
```

The following example shows that how you can insert into nested tables, Where the region is 'Asia' one content is added into dept_names column(which is based on table type).

```
INSERT INTO TABLE (SELECT dept_names
                    FROM    depts
                    WHERE   region = 'Asia')
VALUES          ('Sales'
                )
    /

    Output
    1 record created
```

The following example shows you how you can update nested tables, in the row where region is 'Americas' the value 'Finance' in the dept_names is updated to 'Payroll'.

```
UPDATE TABLE (SELECT dept_names
                FROM    depts
                WHERE   region = 'Americas')
SET column_value = 'Payroll'
WHERE   column_value = 'Finance'
    /
Output
1 Row updated
```

The following example shows you how you can delete a particular value from dept_names column.

```
DELETE FROM TABLE (SELECT dept_names
                   FROM    depts
                   WHERE   region = 'Asia')
WHERE        column_value = 'Payroll'
   /
Output
1 row deleted
```

In the following example the use of database table type is shown, first an object type is generated, because the nested table contains more than one column so object type is used to generate the table type, after creating table type a PL/SQL block is generated to use the table type, in the block a variable is declared of the database table type.
In the executable section the collection (table variable) is initialized, Extended and values are given; at last the values in the collection are printed.
All the functionalities are similar to that of PL/SQL table type's instead that after extending the collection the collection must be initialized with values for first row.

```
CREATE TYPE add_type AS OBJECT (
   street   VARCHAR2 (50),
   city     VARCHAR2 (20)
);
   /

CREATE TYPE add_type_tb AS TABLE OF add_type;
   /
```

Note: that you can not use %ROWTYPE in nested table's datatype.

```
--Use of database table type
DECLARE
   v_add_type    add_type_tb;
BEGIN
   v_add_type                        := add_type_tb ();
   v_add_type.EXTEND;
   --unlike local pl/sql collections,
   --these collection must be first initialized like following
   v_add_type (v_add_type.LAST)    := add_type ('street1', 'karachi');
   DBMS_OUTPUT.put_line (v_add_type (1).street || ' ' || v_add_type (1).city);
END;
/
Output
```
street1 karachi
PL/SQL procedure successfully completed.

Following example show the use of nested table with SQL statements, 10 rows are inserted into the nested table and then value in the nested table are extracted by using a cursor v_add_cur.
Note: that whenever a nested table is used with SQL statements TABLE function is used which makes the nested table to be treated as database table.

```
--table variable base on database table type is used in SQL statement
DECLARE
    v_add_type     add_type_tb;
    v_city         VARCHAR2 (50);
    v_street       VARCHAR2 (50);

    CURSOR v_add_cur
    IS
        SELECT *
        FROM   TABLE (v_add_type);
BEGIN
    v_add_type     := add_type_tb ();

    FOR i IN 1 .. 10
    LOOP
        v_add_type.EXTEND;
        v_add_type (v_add_type.LAST)      := add_type ('street' || i, 'karachi');
    END LOOP;

    FOR v_add_rec IN v_add_cur
    LOOP
        DBMS_OUTPUT.put_line (v_add_rec.street || ' ' || v_add_rec.city);
    END LOOP;
END;
/
Output
street1 karachi
street2 karachi
street3 karachi
street4 karachi
street5 karachi
street6 karachi
street7 karachi
street8 karachi
street9 karachi
street10 karachi
PL/SQL procedure successfully completed.
```

Varrays

The VARRAYs can be used in the similar way as nested tables.
VARRAYs contain a fix number of elements and contain a sequential numbers as
subscript. The use of VARRAY is not as flexible as that of nested tables.

Syntax

CREATE TYPE type_name IS VARRAY (size) OF datatype‖object type;

CREATE TYPE indicates that it is type that is going to generate, type_name is the name of the type,
IS VARRAY indicates that it is VARRAY that is going to generate, data type is used to give a data
type if the VARRAY contains only one column, and if VARRAY contains more than one column
then object type is first created.

The following example creates a VARRAY by using same object type add_type.

Example 1

```
--Creation of varrray
CREATE TYPE add_type_var IS VARRAY (50) OF add_type
/
```

The following example is same as above except that in this VARRAY is used.

```
--use of VARRAY
DECLARE
    v_add_type      add_type_var;
    v_city          VARCHAR2 (50);
    v_street        VARCHAR2 (50);

    CURSOR v_add_cur
    IS
        SELECT *
        FROM    TABLE (v_add_type);
BEGIN
    v_add_type      := add_type_var ();

    FOR i IN 1 .. 10
    LOOP
        v_add_type.EXTEND;
        v_add_type (v_add_type.LAST)      := add_type ('street' || i, 'karachi');
    END LOOP;

    FOR v_add_rec IN v_add_cur
    LOOP
        DBMS_OUTPUT.put_line (v_add_rec.street || ' ' || v_add_rec.city);

    END LOOP;
END;
```

```
street1 karachi
street2 karachi
street3 karachi
street4 karachi
street5 karachi
street6 karachi
street7 karachi
street8 karachi
street9 karachi
street10 karachi
PL/SQL procedure successfully completed.
```

DML operations are not similar in a table having a column of VARRAY type and in a table having a column of Nested table type.

In a table having a column of VARRAY type you cannot update individual elements of a VARRAY column, you have to manipulate whole VARRAY in a pl/sql block and update whole VARRAY.

The following example creates a table having one column v_address of VARRAY type, inserts one row into table and performs updating in a PL/SQL block.

```
--Table creation with one column of VARRAY type
CREATE TABLE test_table(v_id NUMBER,v_address add_type_var);
/
Output
Type created

--insertion into the table
INSERT INTO test_table
VALUES       (1,
              add_type_var (add_type ('street 1', 'karachi'))
             )
/
Output
1 row inserted

--Can not update with this statement
--that was used with columns based on
--nested tables
--It will give the following error
--ORA-25015: cannot perform DML on this nested table view column
UPDATE TABLE (SELECT v_address
              FROM   test_table
              WHERE  v_id = 1)
SET city = 'Hyderabad'
/
Output
set city='Hyderabad'
    *
ERROR at line 2:
ORA-25015: cannot perform DML on this nested table view column

--Updation into the table that have one column of Varray type
DECLARE
```

```
    l_address    add_type_var
                            := add_type_var (add_type ('street 1', 'hyderabad'));
BEGIN
    UPDATE test_table
    SET v_address = l_address
    WHERE  v_id = 1;
END;
/
Output
PL/SQL procedure successfully completed
```

Summary

In this chapter you have learned that an object type is a user defined composite data type representing a data structure and functions and procedures to manipulate the data, The advantage of declaring the nested table types at data base level is that the variables of nested table that are declared in the PL/SQL block can be used in SQL statements, VARRAY have a fixed number of elements and contain sequential numbers as subscript, VARRAYs are not as flexible as nested tables.

Exercise

1. Use the following statements to create a table and insert rows

```
--Example of a simple Table and data insertion into it
CREATE TABLE trad_table(deptno NUMBER(10), empno NUMBER(10),ename
VARCHAR2(30),gender VARCHAR2(8));
INSERT INTO trad_table
VALUES        (1,1,'FARHAN','MALE');
INSERT INTO trad_table
VALUES        (1,2,'ALIZA','FEMALE');
INSERT INTO trad_table
VALUES        (1,3,'IMRAN','MALE');
```

The fields above EMPNO, ENAME and gender are related to employee so make a database object for these three columns to logically group them and perform above insertions, also write statements for selections and update.

2. Use the above created object to declare a PL/SQL variable and do some manipulations.

3. Give an example of Member Method.

4. Give an example of static method.

5. Create one table to achieve the functionality of two tables emp and dept, so that we can perform DML and query records from one table without joining two table through primary and foreign key.
   Insert few records, update records and query records.

6. Execute the following statements and investigate the problem that causes error, "Subscript out of limit"?

```
--Creation of varrray
CREATE TYPE add_type_var IS VARRAY (10) OF add_type
/


--use of VARRAY
DECLARE
    v_add_type    add_type_var;
    v_city        VARCHAR2 (50);
    v_street      VARCHAR2 (50);

    CURSOR v_add_cur
    IS
        SELECT *


FROM    TABLE (v_add_type);
BEGIN
    v_add_type    := add_type_var ();
```

```
    FOR i IN 1 .. 15
    LOOP
       v_add_type.EXTEND;
       v_add_type (v_add_type.LAST)      := add_type ('street' || i, 'karachi');
    END LOOP;

    FOR v_add_rec IN v_add_cur
    LOOP
       DBMS_OUTPUT.put_line (v_add_rec.street || ' ' || v_add_rec.city);
    END LOOP;
END;
/
```

18 BULK SQL

In this chapter you will learn about

Bulk SQL
FORALL statements
Working with sparse collections
Save exceptions with FORALL statements
Bulk collect clause with SELECT and FETCH statements

Introduction

Any SQL statement (Insert, update, delete) written in pl/sql, causes context switching from PL/SQL engine to SQL engine.
For example in pl/sql block 10 rows are inserted in a table as following

```
--inserts 10 rows in test table
/*For using this example create table in scott user
  By using "CREATE TABLE test(v_counter number)"*/
BEGIN
   FOR i IN 1 .. 10
   LOOP
      INSERT INTO TEST (v_counter)
      VALUES        (i);
   END LOOP;
END;
```

In the above Example context switching happens 10 times.
To avoid this context switching PL/SQL uses BULK SQL so that context switching occurs only once.

There are two features for BULK SQL

1. FORALL Statement
2. BULK COLLECT clause

FORALL Statement

Syntax
FORALL counter lower_limit..upper_limit SQL_STATEMENT[SAVE EXCEPTIONS]

INDICE OF collection_name

VALUES OF collection_name

FORALL Statement sends SQL Statements to oracle server in batches bulk of one at a time.
Consider the following statement

Example 1

```
--inserts 10000 rows in test table
/*For using this example create table in scott user
  By using CREATE TABLE test(v_counter number), Create a
Table TEST with one column counter of NUMBER datatype to execute
This example*/

SET TIMING ON

BEGIN
    FOR i IN 1 .. 10000
    LOOP
       INSERT INTO TEST
                    (v_counter
                    )
       VALUES       (i
                    );
    END LOOP;
END;
/
Output
Real: 875
PL/SQL procedure successfully completed
```

**Note: that SET TIMING ON give the elapsed time of a query in milli seconds, you should use
SET TIMING OFF at the end of testing.**

The above Statement can be written for bulk insert but in the values clause one cannot refer loop
counter directly so a table type is created and data is inserted in it first and then it is used in the values
clause of insert Statement within FORALL. Inserting data in PL/SQL table takes very small time.
You can view that in these small programs the following one that uses FORALL is almost three times
faster than the above.

```
--use of FORALL Statement
DECLARE
```

```
     TYPE v_tab_type IS TABLE OF NUMBER
         INDEX BY BINARY_INTEGER;

     v_tab    v_tab_type;
BEGIN
   FOR i IN 1 .. 10000
   LOOP
      v_tab (i)      := i;
   END LOOP;

   FORALL j IN 1 .. 10000
      INSERT INTO TEST
                   (v_counter
                   )
      VALUES       (v_tab (j)
                   );
END;
/

Output
Real: 375
PL/SQL procedure successfully completed
```

Example 2

Following example is same as previous one, only the difference is that both FOR LOOP and FORALL are in one Statement so you can differentiate between the performances of both at same time.

```
DECLARE
    TYPE v_tab_type IS TABLE OF NUMBER
        INDEX BY BINARY_INTEGER;

    v_tab        v_tab_type;
    start_time   NUMBER;
    end_time     NUMBER;
BEGIN

/*The DBMS_UTILITY.GET_TIME built-in function returns the number of hundredths of
seconds(milli seconds) that have elapsed since an arbitrary point in time, can be
an alternative of SET TIMING ON*/

    start_time    := DBMS_UTILITY.get_time;

    FOR i IN 1 .. 100000
    LOOP


INSERT INTO TEST
                   (v_counter
                   )
    VALUES         (i
                   );
    END LOOP;
```

```
end_time         := DBMS_UTILITY.get_time;
DBMS_OUTPUT.put_line (    'FOR LOOP taken '
                          || (end_time - start_time)
                          || ' milliseconds'
                     );
start_time       := DBMS_UTILITY.get_time;

FOR i IN 1 .. 100000
LOOP
   v_tab (i)      := i;
END LOOP;

FORALL j IN 1 .. 100000
   INSERT INTO TEST
                (v_counter
                )
   VALUES       (v_tab (j)
                );
end_time         := DBMS_UTILITY.get_time;
DBMS_OUTPUT.put_line (    'FORALL taken '
                          || (end_time - start_time)
                          || ' milliseconds'
                     );
END;
/
```

Output
FOR LOOP taken 547 milliseconds
FORALL taken 27 milliseconds
PL/SQL procedure successfully completed.

Sparse collection

Syntax

INDICE OF collection_name
VALUES OF collection_name

INDICES OF clause or VALUES OF clause allow the FORALL syntax to be used with sparse collections, deleting some elements from the collection makes it sparse collection.
In the following example the PL/SQL table is assigned values from 1 to 300 in a loop and then two elements are deleted to make it a sparse collection and then INDICES OF clause is used.

Example 1

```
DECLARE
    TYPE v_tab IS TABLE OF NUMBER;

    v_table    v_tab := v_tab ();
BEGIN
--Clear the test table
    DELETE FROM TEST;

--Assign values from 1 to 300 to v_tab
    FOR i IN 1 .. 300
    LOOP
       v_table.EXTEND;
       v_table (v_table.LAST)    := i;
    END LOOP;

--Delete values 101 and 201 from v_tab to make it sparse collection
    v_table.DELETE (101);
    v_table.DELETE (201);

--This will fail becouse there are gaps(sparse collection)

/*forall i in v_table.first..v_table.last
insert into v_table1 values(v_table(i));*/

--this will work fine
    FORALL i IN INDICES OF v_table
       INSERT INTO TEST
       VALUES      (v_table (i)
                   );
END;
/
```
Output
PL/SQL procedure successfully completed

VALUES OF clause allow looping through a table by using the elements of another table. If the collection is sparse and it needs to loop through only some specific elements then use VALUES OF clause.

In the following example the values of v_table plsql table are inserted into test1 table by looping through the elements of v_table1 PL/SQL table.

Example 1

```
--Use of VALUE OF clause
--Create another table first by using following Statement
--Create table test1 as select * from test;

DECLARE
    TYPE v_tab IS TABLE OF VARCHAR2 (50);

    TYPE v_tab1 IS TABLE OF PLS_INTEGER;

    v_table     v_tab  := v_tab ();
    v_table1    v_tab1 := v_tab1 ();
BEGIN
--Clear tables
    DELETE FROM test1;

--Assign values to each table
    FOR i IN 1 .. 300
    LOOP
        v_table.EXTEND;
        v_table (v_tablc.LAST)      := i;

        IF MOD (i, 100) = 0
        THEN
            v_table1.EXTEND;
            v_table1 (v_table1.LAST)     := i;
        END IF;
    END LOOP;

--Make sparse collection
    v_table.DELETE (101);
    v_table.DELETE (201);
    FORALL i IN VALUES OF v_table1
        INSERT INTO test1
        VALUES          (v_table (i));
    COMMIT; END;
/
Output PL/SQL Procedure successfully completed
```

Save Exceptions

By default if any row of FORALL loop raises an exception, all changes a roll backed and statement terminates but by using 'Save Exceptions' Loop continues to execute and saves the exceptions. Further action with the exceptions can be taken in the Exception Section.

SQL%BULK_EXCEPTIONS is a complex data type (record) with two fields: ERROR_INDEX is the iteration that caused the error, and ERROR_CODE is the Oracle error message number describing the error.

In the following Example SAVE EXCEPTION is used, V_TAB is of varchar2 type, in v_tab at 8th value is replaced by 8e so when inserting into test table it raises exception -24381(Not a valid number), because v_counter column of test table has number data type.

An exception has been defined and associated with the error number -24381.

Finally in the Exception section the error is trapped.

Example 1

```
--BULK EXCEPTION handling
DECLARE
    TYPE v_tab_type IS TABLE OF VARCHAR2 (15)
        INDEX BY BINARY_INTEGER;

    v_tab           v_tab_type;
    e_exp           EXCEPTION;
    PRAGMA EXCEPTION_INIT (e_exp, -24381);
    v_err_count     NUMBER;
    v_err_code      NUMBER;
    v_err_msg       VARCHAR2 (500);
BEGIN
    FOR i IN 1 .. 10
    LOOP
        v_tab (i)       := i;
    END LOOP;

    v_tab (8)       := '8e';
    FORALL j IN 1 .. 10 SAVE EXCEPTIONS
        INSERT INTO TEST
                    (v_counter
                    )
        VALUES      (v_tab (j)
                    );
EXCEPTION
    WHEN e_exp
    THEN
        v_err_count     := SQL%BULK_EXCEPTIONS.COUNT;

        FOR i IN 1 .. v_err_count
        LOOP


            v_err_code      := SQL%BULK_EXCEPTIONS (i).ERROR_CODE * -1;
            v_err_msg       := SQLERRM (v_err_code);
```

```
        DBMS_OUTPUT.put_line (    'Error aquired at '
                            || v_tab (SQL%BULK_EXCEPTIONS (i).ERROR_INDEX)
                            || ' Error_code='
                            || v_err_code
                            || ' Error_msg='
                            || v_err_msg
                          );
     END LOOP;
END;
/

Output
Error acquired at 8e Error_code=-1722 Error_msg=ORA-01722: invalid number
PL/SQL procedure successfully completed.
```

BULK COLLECT clause

Syntax

SELECT columns
BULK COLLECT INTO Table type variable
FROM table_name;

BULK COLLECT clause is used to fetch bunch of records from database at once.

In the following example a PL/SQL table v_emp is created and records are inserted by using bulk collect.
BULK COLLECT returns rows in bulk so only PL/SQL tables can be used to store returned records. Nested Table is initialized before use and EXTEND method is used before assigning a value but when Nested Tables are used with BULK COLLECT , they are automatically get initialized and EXTEND method is not required as well.

Example 1

```
--use of BULK COLLECT Clause
DECLARE
    TYPE v_emp_type IS TABLE OF EMP%ROWTYPE;

    v_emp    v_emp_type;
BEGIN
    SELECT *
    BULK COLLECT INTO v_emp
    FROM    EMP;

    FOR i IN v_emp.FIRST .. v_emp.LAST
    LOOP
        DBMS_OUTPUT.put_line (    'EMP_NO='
                            || v_emp (i).empno
                            || '      EMP_Name='
                            || v_emp (i).ename
                        );
    END LOOP;
END;
/
```

BULK COLLECT is also used with FETCH statement

Syntax
FETCH cursor_name BULLECT COLLECT INTO table_name LIMIT limit_number;

LIMIT is an optional parameter which specifies that how many numbers of records are fetched at once.
The advantage of using BULK COLLECT with Fetch clause is that LIMIT parameter can be used. In the following example loop for printing the elements of v_emp are used inside the FETCH LOOP, it is because when it fetch 2nd 100 records it replaces 1st 100 records and when fetching 3rd 100 records it replace 2nd 100 records so if the inner loop is given out of FETCH LOOP it prints only last 100 records.

Example 1

```
DECLARE
    CURSOR c_emp
    IS
        SELECT *
        FROM    emp;

    TYPE v_emp_type IS TABLE OF emp%ROWTYPE;

    v_emp    v_emp_type;
BEGIN
    OPEN c_emp;

    LOOP
        FETCH c_emp
        BULK COLLECT INTO v_emp LIMIT 100;

        EXIT WHEN v_emp.COUNT = 0;

        FOR i IN v_emp.FIRST .. v_emp.LAST
        LOOP
            DBMS_OUTPUT.put_line (v_emp (i).empno || ' ' || v_emp (i).ename);
        END LOOP;
    END LOOP;

    CLOSE c_emp;
END;
/
```

Dynamic SQL can be used with BULK COLLECT

Example 1

```
--BULK COLLECT with dynamic sql
DECLARE
    TYPE forall_type IS TABLE OF NUMBER;

    v_forall        forall_type := forall_type (120, 1234, 145);
    bulk_excep    EXCEPTION;
    PRAGMA EXCEPTION_INIT (bulk_excep, -24381);
BEGIN
    FORALL i IN 1 .. v_forall.COUNT SAVE EXCEPTIONS
        EXECUTE IMMEDIATE --Dynamic sql
                        'INSERT INTO test
    VALUES        (:v_val)'
    USING             v_forall (i);
EXCEPTION
    WHEN bulk_excep
    THEN
        FOR i IN 1 .. SQL%BULK_EXCEPTIONS.COUNT
        LOOP
            DBMS_OUTPUT.put_line (    SQL%BULK_EXCEPTIONS (i).ERROR_INDEX
                                || ' '
                                || SQLERRM
                                            ( -1
                                             * SQL%BULK_EXCEPTIONS(i).ERROR_CODE));
        END LOOP;
END;
/
```

BULK COLLECT can also be used with INSERT, UPDATE and DELETE statements with conjunction to RETURNING clause as explained in the following examples.

Example 1

```
--Bulk collect with Delete
--Make sure that Test table is not empty
--Output depend upon number of rows deleted
--Deletion example
DECLARE
    TYPE v_num_type IS TABLE OF NUMBER
        INDEX BY BINARY_INTEGER;

    v_num    v_num_type;
BEGIN
    DELETE FROM TEST
    RETURNING    v_counter
    BULK COLLECT INTO v_num;

    DBMS_OUTPUT.put_line ('Rows deleted: ' || SQL%ROWCOUNT);

    FOR i IN v_num.FIRST .. v_num.LAST
    LOOP
        DBMS_OUTPUT.put_line ('Row ' || v_num (i));
    END LOOP;
END;
/

Output
Rows deleted: 4
Row 1
Row 2
Row 3
Row 4
PL/SQL Procedure successfully completed
```

Example 2

```
--Update table test with BULK COLLECT
--Make sure that v_counter=2 row exists in test table
--Updation example
DECLARE
    TYPE v_num_type IS TABLE OF NUMBER
        INDEX BY BINARY_INTEGER;

    v_num      v_num_type;
BEGIN
    UPDATE      TEST
    SET v_counter = 1
    WHERE       v_counter = 2
    RETURNING v_counter
    BULK COLLECT INTO v_num;

    DBMS_OUTPUT.put_line ('Rows deleted: ' || SQL%ROWCOUNT);

    FOR i IN v_num.FIRST .. v_num.LAST
    LOOP
        DBMS_OUTPUT.put_line ('Row ' || v_num (i));
    END LOOP;
END;
/
```

```
Output
Rows deleted: 1
Row 1
PL/SQL Procedure successfully completed
```

Summary

In this chapter you have learned about BULK SQL, FORALL Statement sends SQL Statements to oracle server in batches bulk of one at a time that is much faster than the traditional loops, Bulk collect clause can be used with SQL Select statement or with Fetch statements to select the statements in bunches, indices of clause is used to loop through sparse collection, Values of clause is used to insert data of one collection by using the indexes of other collection, You have an option Save exceptions with FORALL statements to run the statement successfully and save the exceptions.

Exercise

1. Create a PLSQL block that takes all data from EMP table and inserts it into new table say emp_test by using BULK SQL.
   Create another PLSQL block that takes all data from EMP table and inserts it into new Table, say emp_test without using BULK SQL, Compare the time between the two.

2. Create the above PL/SQL block to handle exceptions, change the EMP table's column Empno_test to Varchar2, and change any EMPNO in emp_test table with char value. Create another table emp_test2 that should be a copy of previous EMP table. Because EMPNO is number column in emp_test2 so it will cause an exception at the particulr row while inserting data from emp_test1.

3. Correct the following statement

```
DECLARE
    TYPE v_num_type IS TABLE OF NUMBER
        INDEX BY BINARY_INTEGER;
    v_num    v_num_type;
BEGIN
    UPDATE    TEST
    SET v_counter = 1
    WHERE       v_counter = 2
    RETURNING v_counter;
    DBMS_OUTPUT.put_line ('Rows deleted: ' || SQL%ROWCOUNT);
    FOR i IN v_num.FIRST .. v_num.LAST
    LOOP
        DBMS_OUTPUT.put_line ('Row ' || v_num (i));
    END LOOP;
END;
/
```

19 DYNAMIC SQL

In this chapter you will learn about

What is dynamic SQL?
EXECUTE IMMEDIATE statement
The INTO and USING clause
RETURNING INTO clause
Cursor variables

What is dynamic SQL?

Dynamic SQL is used to construct the SQL statements at runtime.
For example a procedure takes EMPNO as input and returns ENAME, SAL. Each time an input parameter is passed it returns ENAME and SAL, there can be different data only, this type of statements are called static, Now if there is a requirement that if the EMPNO=50 then return ENAME, SAL, HIREDATE and comm., than you need to build dynamic SQL statement.
Dynamic SQL is very useful for reports and for scripting languages like ASP. In dynamic SQL a string containing complete Statement is provided by the user and is executed by using the command EXECUTE IMMEDIATE, the string can contain different statements in each execution as following

```
EXECUTE IMMEDIATE 'select deptno,dename from dept';
EXECUTE IMMEDIATE 'select deptno,dename,loc from dept';
EXECUTE IMMEDIATE 'select empno,ename from emp';
```

Execute Immediate

The SQL Statements and PLSQL blocks are parsed and executed by EXECUTE_IMMEDIATE Statement at run time.

Syntax

EXECUTE IMMEDIATE sql_string
[INTO defined_variable1, defined_variable2,...]
[USING [IN|OUT|IN OUT] bind_argument1, bind_argument2...]
[{RETURNING|RETURN} field1, field2, INTO bind_argument1, bind_argument2 ...]

Sql_string is the string that contains the SQL statement or PL/SQL block that needs to execute at run time.

The INTO clause is used to hold the values returned by select statement's columns for single row. USING clause contains arguments that are passed to the statements, IN, OUT or IN OUT can be the mode of arguments. RETURNING INTO or RETURN clause contain the bind arguments which hold the values retuned by SQL statement or PL/SQL blocks.
RETURNING INTO clause can contain bind arguments for any mode, default mode is OUT.

In the following example the EXECUTE IMMEDIATE statement executes the Statements of V_SRTING variable, V_SRTING takes Statements from substitution variable at run time, have a look at the following example and execute the block.
After executing PL/SQL block provide the following as substitution variable's value at SQL prompt.

```
CREATE   TABLE dynamic_tab(v_col1 NUMBER,v_col2 VARCHAR2(10))
```

Note: the no semicolon is provided at the end of the statement.
After successfully executing the block, run the describe command at sql prompt as

```
    DESC dynamic_tab
```

It shows the structure of the table created at run time, after that execute the PLSQL block again with the following as substitution variable's value

```
    DROP TABLE dynamic_tab
```

After run the describe command again, because the table has been dropped so it gives an error that the object does not exist.

```
Example 1

--Dynamic Sql
DECLARE
   v_string    VARCHAR2 (200) := '&P_STRING';
BEGIN
   EXECUTE IMMEDIATE v_string;
END;
/

Output
PL/SQL Procedure successfully completed
```

This example briefly introduced the purpose of dynamic sql.
The DDL statements cannot have a bind argument.

The INTO and USING clause

The INTO clause and USING clause are defined earlier, the following example explains their usage in detail, have a look at the example below and execute it.

After executing the following PL/SQL block this string is given at SQL prompt for substitution variable P_STRING

```
SELECT ENAME INTO :ENAME FROM EMP WHERE EMPNO=:EMPNO
```

Then any value is given for the P_EMPNO substitution variable that is used in the where clause of the dynamic string, the value is for example 8888.
The PL/SQL block will execute the dynamic string, in the where clause the: EMPNO argument is used, the value assigned to P_EMPNO substitution variable is used in the argument as P_EMPNO is used in USING clause.
The variable V_NAME gets the ENAME as it is used in INTO clause and is printed to the screen.
Note: that bind arguments used in the dynamic string can be of any name, character or number but must be prefixed by colon as :A, :EMPANO, :1.

Create another table emp_test having similar structure and data as of EMP table.
Execute the PL/SQL block again with the following dynamic string

```
SELECT ENAME FROM EMP_TEST WHERE EMPNO=:A
```

Provide the EMPNO for the substitution variable say 9898, Note that the PL/SQL block successfully executes and returns the result thought the INTO clause is not specified in the string, It mean that INTO clause is not necessary in the dynamic string.

Example 1

```
DECLARE
    v_string    VARCHAR2 (200)  := '&P_String';
    v_name      VARCHAR2 (30);
    p_empno     NUMBER          := &p_empno;
BEGIN
    EXECUTE IMMEDIATE v_string
    INTO                v_name
    USING               p_empno;

    DBMS_OUTPUT.put_line ('Employee is ' || v_name);
END;
/
```

RETURNING INTO clause

The following example shows the usage of RETURNING INTO clause,
It is similar to the INTO clause as a variable is used to get the values that what is the new updated
value, Run the PL/SQL block and provide 9898 for substitution variable of P_EMPNO.

Example 1

```
--Usage of RETURNING INTO clause
DECLARE
    v_string    VARCHAR2 (200);
    v_empno     NUMBER          := '&p_empno';
    v_ename     VARCHAR2 (30);
BEGIN
    v_string    :=
       'UPDATE EMP SET ENAME=''Farhan'' where empno=:EMNO RETURNING ENAME INTO
:ENM';

    EXECUTE IMMEDIATE v_string
    USING              v_empno
    RETURNING INTO     v_ename;

    DBMS_OUTPUT.put_line ('New name ' || v_ename);
END;
/
Output
Enter value for p_empno: 7902
old   4:    v_empno    NUMBER           := '&p_empno';
new   4:    v_empno    NUMBER           := '7902';
New name Farhan
PL/SQL procedure successfully completed.
```

**Note that when EXECUTE IMMEDIATE contain both USING clause and RETURNING
INTO clause, the USING clause can only contain IN argument.**

The following example creates a procedure del_rows and uses the dynamic SQL to provide the table
name and where clause condition at run time.
When executing the procedure the table name and where clause condition is provided as arguments
and it deletes the rows satisfying the where clause, if the where clause condition is not provided then
this procedure raises and error.
After creating the procedure call the procedure as following

```
Exec del_rows('emp','empno=7900');
```
This deletes the row of employee number 7900 from EMP table.

```
Example 2
```

```
CREATE OR REPLACE PROCEDURE del_rows (
    tab_name     IN    VARCHAR2,
    condition    IN    VARCHAR2 DEFAULT NULL
)
AS
    where_clause    VARCHAR2 (100) := ' WHERE ' || condition;
BEGIN
    IF condition IS NULL
    THEN
        raise_application_error (-20050, 'You must provide the condiction');
    END IF;

    EXECUTE IMMEDIATE 'DELETE FROM ' || tab_name || where_clause;
END;
/

Output
PL/SQL procedure successfully completed
```

Cursor variables or ref cursor

A cursor variable is used to individually process each row returned by a multiple row query similarly as static cursors.
A *cursor variable* contains a pointer to a query result set; result set is determined by the execution of the OPEN FOR statement.
An extra USING clause is used in OPEN-FOR, FETCH and CLOSE Statements that is optional.

Syntax
OPEN cursor_variable FOR Dynamic_SQL_String [USING bind_argument1, ind_argument2..]

Cursor Variable is a based on a weak REF Cursor type.

Consider the following example in which REF CURSOR type is defined then a Cursor variable emp_ref_cur is defined of that type, at run time v_string gets value from substitution variable.
In the executable section cursor variable emp_ref_cur is opened for v_string, after fetching is done in variables and at the end cursor is closed.

Note that a semicolon is given before LOOP keyword.

Let's say at run time we provide following string

```
    SELECT EMPNO, ENAME FROM EMP
```

The result will be as shown below in output section

```
Example 1

--Usage of refcursor
DECLARE
   TYPE emp_ref_cur_ty IS REF CURSOR;

   emp_ref_cur      emp_ref_cur_ty;
   v_empno          emp.empno%TYPE;
   v_ename          emp.ename%TYPE;
   v_string         VARCHAR2 (200)    := '&P_String';
BEGIN
   OPEN emp_ref_cur FOR v_string;

   LOOP
      FETCH emp_ref_cur
      INTO  v_empno,
            v_ename;

      EXIT WHEN emp_ref_cur%NOTFOUND;
      DBMS_OUTPUT.put_line (v_empno || ' ' || v_ename);
   END LOOP;

   CLOSE emp_ref_cur;
END;
/

Output
7566   FAISAL
7654   MARTIN
7698   BLAKE
7782   SHAHZAD
7788   SCOTT
7839   KINGS
7844   TURNER
7876   ADAMS
7900   JAMES
7902   FORD
9898   TEST

PL/SQL procedure successfully completed.
```

USING Clause is used to specify bind arguments

Following example takes the P_EMPNO through substitution variable and uses it in the using clause that gives this value to bind argument: 1 so the records come only for the EMPNO provided.
At run time following EMPNO is provided for substitution variable 7900.

Example 1

```
--Usage of USING clause
DECLARE
    TYPE emp_ref_cur_ty IS REF CURSOR;

    emp_ref_cur     emp_ref_cur_ty;
    v_empno         emp.empno%TYPE;
    v_ename         emp.ename%TYPE;
    p_empno         NUMBER              := &p_emno;
BEGIN
    OPEN emp_ref_cur FOR 'SELECT empno,ename
                    FROM emp
                    WHERE empno=:1' USING p_empno;

    LOOP
      FETCH emp_ref_cur
      INTO  v_empno,
            v_ename;

      EXIT WHEN emp_ref_cur%NOTFOUND;
      DBMS_OUTPUT.put_line (v_empno || ' ' || v_ename);
    END LOOP;

    CLOSE emp_ref_cur;
END;
/

Output
Enter value for p_emno: 7900
old   6: P_EMPNO NUMBER:=&P_EMNO;
new   6: P_EMPNO NUMBER:=7900;
7900  JAMES

PL/SQL procedure successfully completed.
```

NOTE: RETURN keywod is also used with REF CURSOR but if RETURN keyword is used with REF CURSOR, the cursor can't be used with Dynamic SQL. Normally we use RETURN keyword with REF CURSOR while we make a form's block on a procedure that reurns records by using this REF CURSOR.

Summary

In this chapter you have learned that Dynamic SQL is used to construct SQL and PL/SQL statements at run time, EXECUTE IMMEDIATE is used to execute the dynamic string passed to it, the INTO clause is used to hold the values returned by select statement's columns for single row. USING clause contains arguments that are passed to the statements, IN, OUT or IN OUT can be the mode of arguments. RETURNING INTO or RETURN clause contain the bind arguments which hold the values retuned by SQL statement or PL/SQL blocks, and a cursor variable is used to individually process each row returned by a multiple row query similarly as static cursors.

Exercise

1. Create a simple PL/SQL program that should delete any particular record from EMP table, Use dynamic SQL.

2. What is wrong with the following statement

```
DECLARE
    v_string    VARCHAR2 (200)  := 'select ename from emp';
    v_name      VARCHAR2 (30);
    p_empno     NUMBER          :=7900;
 BEGIN
    EXECUTE IMMEDIATE v_string
    INTO               v_name
    USING              p_empno;
    DBMS_OUTPUT.put_line ('Employee is ' || v_name);
 END;
```

3. Create a PL/SQL block that uses OPEN-FOR, FETCH and CLOSE statements, Give a SQL statement which selects employee name, Salary and commission of the employees whose salary is greater than 1000 by using "USING" clause, Show first original Name, Salary and commission and then increments salary by 1000 and shows the incremented salary.

4. Correct the following statement

```
--Usag of refcursor
DECLARE
    TYPE emp_ref_c_ty IS CURSOR;

    emp_ref_c    emp_ref_c_ty;
    v_empno      emp.empno%TYPE;
    v_ename      emp.ename%TYPE;
    v_string     VARCHAR2 (200)  := '&P_String';
BEGIN
```

```
    OPEN emp_ref_c FOR v_string

  LOOP


      FETCH emp_ref_c
      INTO  v_empno,
            v_ename;

      EXIT WHEN emp_ref_c%NOTFOUND;
      DBMS_OUTPUT.put_line (v_empno || ' ' || v_ename);
  END LOOP;

      CLOSE emp_ref_c;
END;
/
```

20 NEW FEATURES OF PL/SQL IN ORACLE DATABASE 11G

In this chapter you will learn about

New data types SIMPLE_INTEGER, SIMPLE_FLOAT, and SIMPLE_DOUBLE
Continue statement
Sequence in PL/SQL expression
Dynamic SQL enhancements
Named and mixed notation when calling a function from SQL statement
Trigger enhancement
Cross session PL/SQL function result cache
Automatic subprogram inlining
Restriction in FORALL Statements Removed
New compile time warning

1. New SIMPLE data types

New data types SIMPLE_INTEGER, SIMPLE_FLOAT and SIMPLE_DOUBLE are introduced in oracle 11g.
These new data types are subtype of PLS_INTEGER, BINARY_FLOAT and BINARY_DOUBLE rcspcctively.
These subtypes have same range as their base types and have an additional not null constraint.
These data types provide significant performance benefit when the compilation mode is NATIVE; this is because the arithmetic operations for these data types are directly done on hardware layer.
However the performance gain is very small when compilation mode is INTERPERATED as shown following

Example 1

```
--Usage of new data type
DECLARE
    v_var1      simple_integer := 1;
    v_var2      simple_integer := 2;
    v_var3      PLS_INTEGER;
    v_var4      PLS_INTEGER;
    st_time     NUMBER;
    end_time    NUMBER;
BEGIN
    st_time      := DBMS_UTILITY.get_time;

    FOR i IN 1 .. 100000
    LOOP
```

```
v_var2     := v_var1 + v_var2;
   END LOOP;

   end_time     := DBMS_UTILITY.get_time;
   DBMS_OUTPUT.put_line ('Time taken by New datatype ' || end_time - st_time);
   st_time      := DBMS_UTILITY.get_time;

   FOR i IN 1 .. 100000
   LOOP
      v_var4     := v_var3 + v_var4;
   END LOOP;

   end_time     := DBMS_UTILITY.get_time;
   DBMS_OUTPUT.put_line ('Time taken by Old datatype ' || end_time - st_time);
END;
/
```
Output

2. CONTINUE statement

Continue statement is used to post pond a complete iteration or part of iteration of a loop, explained in chapter 4.

3. Sequence in PL/SQL expression

Now sequence can be directly used inside a PL/SQL expression as following

Example 1

```
CREATE SEQUENCE test_seq START WITH 1 INCREMENT BY 1;

BEGIN
   dmbs_output.put_line ('Next available sequence is ' || test_seq.NEXTVAL);
END;
```

4. Dynamic SQL enhancements

Dynamic SQL is covered in chapter 19.
DBMS_SQL package now supports all data types that Native dynamic SQL supports and two new functions
DBMS_SQL.REF_CURSOR and DBMS_SQL.TO_CURSOR_NUMBER are introduced to switch between native dynamic SQL and DBMS_SQL package.

5. Named and mixed notation when calling a function from SQL statement

Now Named and mixed notation is allowed when the function is called within SQL statement, previously positional notation was allowed only.

Example 1

```
--Function to show the mixed notation usage in SQL expressions
CREATE OR REPLACE FUNCTION sql_exp_proc (p_val1 NUMBER, p_val2 NUMBER)
    RETURN NUMBER
IS
BEGIN
    RETURN (p_val1 + p_val2);
END;
/

--Positional notation, Previously allowed only
SELECT sql_exp_proc (1, 2)
FROM   DUAL
/
--Mixed notation, was not allowed previously
SELECT sql_exp_proc (p_val1 => 1, 2)
FROM   DUAL
/
```

6. Trigger enhancement

ENABLE, DISABLE and FOLLOWS options are introduced in 11G, covered in chapter 16.

7. Compound triggers

A new type of trigger is introduced called compound trigger, which combines all the statement and row trigger within one trigger, covered in detail in chapter 14.

8. PL/SQL compiler can now generate native code directly

Previously PL/SQL code was translated into C code which was then converted to native code, now the code is directly converted to native code when parameter PL/SQL_CODE_TYPE is set to 'NATIVE'.

9. Cross session PL/SQL function result cache

A result cached function is a function whose parameter and returned values are stored in the cache, each time the function is called with same parameter values the function is invoked from cache.
The cache was made session wise, means if a user invokes a function with same parameter values as previously called, the function is called from cache ,only if the function was previously called in the same cache.

Oracle 11g now supports cross session cache means the result of a function and its parameter values are stored in shared global area (SGA) and is available to any session.
Following example shows the usage of result cached function

```
--Result cached function
CREATE OR REPLACE PACKAGE result_cached_pkg
AS
    TYPE emp_typ IS TABLE OF emp%ROWTYPE
       INDEX BY BINARY_INTEGER;

   FUNCTION result_cached_fun (p_emp NUMBER)
      RETURN NUMBER;
  result_cache;
END;
/

CREATE OR REPLACE PACKAGE BODY result_cached_pkg
AS
    FUNCTION result_cached_fun (p_emp NUMBER)
       RETURN NUMBER
    result_cache
    relies_on(emp)
    IS

  v_emp    emp_ty;
```

```
    BEGIN
        SELECT *
        INTO    v_emp
        FROM    emp
        WHERE   empno = p_emp;
    END;
END;
/
```

10.　　Automatic subprogram inlining

When a subprogram is called in a program it takes a noticeable performance overhead, especially when a subprogram is called inside a loop so the solution is not to replace the subprograms calls with their code as it will be against the modular programming, one solution of this problem is automatic subprogram inlinning.
When a subprogram is called with automatic subprogram inlinning enabled, a copy of the subprogram is maintained at the calling place, you can understand more with following syntax

CREATE OR REPLCAE PROCEDURE p_calling_procedure
IS
BEGIN

STATEMENT 1;
STATEMENT 2;
-----suppose here is code of 1000 lines

END;

BEGIN
LOOP
p_calling_procedure;
END LOOP;
END;

When the subprogram inlining is enabled the compiler will create the calling program as following

Example 1

BEGIN

LOOP

```
STATEMENT 1;
STATEMENT 2;
P_calling_procedure; --A logical copy of the procedure is maintained here with code

END LOOP;

END;
```

Note: subprogram code is written inside calling program directly; this is just a supposed image to make you understand that how subprogram inlinning works.
Subprogram inlinning can be turned on by using two methods

SET PL_SQL_OPTIMIZE_LEVEL to 3
or
PRAGMA INLINE compiler directive

An example is shown below, first example is without subprogram inlining, and second one is with subprogram inlining

```
ALTER SESSION SET plsql_optimize_level=2;

SET SERVEROUTPUT ON

DECLARE
    l_loops     NUMBER := 10000000;
    l_start     NUMBER;
    l_return    NUMBER;

    FUNCTION add_numbers (p_1 IN NUMBER, p_2 IN NUMBER)
        RETURN NUMBER
    AS
    BEGIN
        RETURN p_1 + p_2;
    END add_numbers;
BEGIN
    l_start     := DBMS_UTILITY.get_time;

    FOR i IN 1 .. l_loops
    LOOP
        --PRAGMA INLINE (add_numbers, 'YES');
        l_return    := add_numbers (1, i);
    END LOOP;

    DBMS_OUTPUT.put_line (   'Elapsed Time: '
                         || (DBMS_UTILITY.get_time - l_start)
                         || ' hsecs'

                         );
END;
```

Elapsed Time: 509 hsecs
PL/SQL procedure successfully completed.

```
ALTER SESSION SET plsql_optimize_level=2;

SET SERVEROUTPUT ON

DECLARE
    l_loops     NUMBER := 10000000;
    l_start     NUMBER;
    l_return    NUMBER;

    FUNCTION add_numbers (p_1 IN NUMBER, p_2 IN NUMBER)
        RETURN NUMBER
    AS
    BEGIN
        RETURN p_1 + p_2;
    END add_numbers;
BEGIN
    l_start     := DBMS_UTILITY.get_time;

    FOR i IN 1 .. l_loops
    LOOP
    PRAGMA INLINE (add_numbers, 'YES');
        l_return    := add_numbers (1, i);
    END LOOP;

    DBMS_OUTPUT.put_line (   'Elapsed Time: '
                          || (DBMS_UTILITY.get_time - l_start)
                          || ' hsecs'
                         );
END;
/
```
Elapsed Time: 245 hsecs
PL/SQL procedure successfully completed.

------------------------- --------------------------------------- --------------------------------

PLS-00436 Restriction in FORALL Statements Removed

The PLS-00436 restriction has been removed, which means you can now reference the individual elements of a collection within the SET and WHERE clauses of a DML statement in a FORALL construct. To see this in action, create and populates a test table using the following code.

```
CREATE TABLE forall_test (
 id          NUMBER,
 description VARCHAR2(50)
);

INSERT INTO forall_test VALUES (1, 'ONE');
INSERT INTO forall_test VALUES (2, 'TWO');
INSERT INTO forall_test VALUES (3, 'THREE');
INSERT INTO forall_test VALUES (4, 'FOUR');
INSERT INTO forall_test VALUES (5, 'FIVE');
COMMIT;


------------------------


DECLARE
 TYPE t_forall_test_tab IS TABLE OF forall_test%ROWTYPE;
 l_tab t_forall_test_tab;
BEGIN
 -- Retrieve the existing data into a collection.
 SELECT *
 BULK COLLECT INTO l_tab
 FROM  forall_test;

 -- Alter the data in the collection.
 FOR i IN l_tab.first .. l_tab.last LOOP
  l_tab(i).description := 'Description for ' || i;
 END LOOP;

 -- Update the table using the collection.
 FORALL i IN l_tab.first .. l_tab.last
  UPDATE forall_test
  SET   description = l_tab(i).description
  WHERE  id        = l_tab(i).id;

 COMMIT;
END;
/
```

SELECT * FROM forall_test;

    ID DESCRIPTION

---------- ---------------------------
    1 Description for 1
    2 Description for 2
    3 Description for 3
    4 Description for 4
    5 Description for 5

5 rows selected.

Notice both the SET and WHERE clauses contain references to individual columns in the collection. This makes using bulk-binds for DML even easier as we no longer need to maintain multiple collections if we need to reference columns in the WHERE clause. It can also improve performance of updates, as previous versions required updates of the whole row using the ROW keyword, which included potentially unnecessary updates of primary key and foreign key columns.

PLW-06009 New compile time warning

when raise_application_error or raise is not used inside when-others exception handler.

Summary

In this chapter you have learned about new and enhanced features of PL/SQL in oracle database 11G, new data type SIMPLE_INTEGER, SIMPLE_FLOAT, SIMPLE_DOUBLE are introduced that give performance benefit when the compilation mode is NATIVE because calculation for these data type is done on hardware layer, the CONTINUE statement is used to bypass a complete iteration or part of iteration in a loop,
Sequence can be directly called in PL/SQL expressions now, Now DBMS_SQL package supports all data types that Native dynamic SQL supports, previously only positional notation was allowed when a function was called in SQL expressions but now named or mixed notation can also be used, Now you can enable or disable a trigger at creation time with ENABLE / DISABLE option, Compound triggers can be created to combine different trigger types, now a function's parameter values and result can be cached across session, automatic program inlining helps reducing performance overhead when calling a subprogram, individual elements of a nested table can be called in FORALL statement, new compile time warning is introduce when a raise or raise_application_error is not specified in WHEN_OTHERS.

ANSWERS OF THE EXCERCISES

Chapter 2 General programming language fundamentals

1.

```
Delimiter    >
Literal     'A'
```

2.

Identifier   v_empno

3.

No the maximum length of the identifier can be 30 characters.

Chapter 3 PL/SQL data type

1.
```
--Variable usage
DECLARE
    v_var1    NUMBER (4);
    v_var2    NUMBER (4);
    v_var3    NUMBER (4);
    v_var4    NUMBER (4);
    v_one     NUMBER (4)  := 6;
    v_two     NUMBER (4)  := 3;
BEGIN
    v_var1     := v_one / v_two;
    v_var2     := v_one * v_two;
    v_var3     := v_one + v_two;
    v_var4     := v_one - v_two;
    DBMS_OUTPUT.put_line (    'div '
                         ||  v_var1
                         || ' mult '
                         ||  v_var2
                         || ' add '
                         ||  v_var3
                         || ' subs '
                         ||  v_var4
                         );
END;
/
```

2.
Output will be 4 because when two variables with the same name exist the local gets preference.

3.
Label should be given up on DECLARE keyword like following

```
--label usage
<<outer>>
DECLARE
    v_var1    NUMBER (4) := 2;
BEGIN
    DECLARE
        v_var1    NUMBER (4) := 4;
    BEGIN
        DBMS_OUTPUT.put_line (OUTER.v_var1);
    END;
END;
/
```

4.

The length of the variable is smaller than the assigned value, the length should be minimum 5 for this value.

5.

Use the conversion operator as following

```
--assigned to a number variable
DECLARE
    v_var    NUMBER (10);
BEGIN
    v_var    := TO_NUMBER ('5684');
    DBMS_OUTPUT.put_line (v_var);
END;
/
```

Chapter 4 Interacting with oracle server

1.

```
--SELECT statement inside PL/SQL
DECLARE
    v_empno    NUMBER;
    v_ename    VARCHAR2 (30);
    v_job      VARCHAR2 (27);
    v_mgr      NUMBER;
BEGIN
    SELECT empno,
           ename,
           job,
           mgr
    INTO   v_empno,
           v_ename,
```

```
            v_job,
            v_mgr
    FROM    emp
    WHERE   empno = 7900;

    DBMS_OUTPUT.put_line (v_empno || ' ' || v_ename || ' ' || v_job || ' '||
v_mgr);
END;
/
```

2.

```
--When the record is found it updates else shows
--the message that record does not exists
--You can check by changing the empno
BEGIN
    UPDATE emp
    SET sal = 1500
    WHERE   empno = 78599;

    IF SQL%NOTFOUND
    THEN
        DBMS_OUTPUT.put_line ('Record does not exists');
    END IF;
END;
/
```

Chapter 5 Conditional control statements

1.

```
BEGIN
    IF TO_CHAR (SYSDATE, 'YYYY') = '2009'
    THEN
        DBMS_OUTPUT.put_line ('The year is 2009');
    END IF;
END;
/
```

2.

```
BEGIN
    IF TO_CHAR (SYSDATE, 'YYYY') = '2009'
    THEN
        DBMS_OUTPUT.put_line ('The year is 2009');
    ELSE
        DBMS_OUTPUT.put_line ('The year is NOT 2009');
    END IF;
END;
```

ANSWERS OF THE EXCERCISES

```
/

3.
DECLARE
   v_marks    NUMBER := &marks;
BEGIN
   IF v_marks > 100
   THEN
      DBMS_OUTPUT.put_line ('Invalid number');
   ELSIF v_marks <= 100 AND v_marks >= 80
   THEN
      DBMS_OUTPUT.put_line ('A One Grade');
   ELSIF v_marks < 80 AND v_marks >= 70
   THEN
      DBMS_OUTPUT.put_line ('A Grade');
   ELSIF v_marks < 70 AND v_marks >= 60
   THEN
      DBMS_OUTPUT.put_line ('B GRADE');
   ELSIF v_marks < 60
   THEN
      DBMS_OUTPUT.put_line ('FAIL');
   ELSE
      DBMS_OUTPUT.put_line ('Invalid number');
   END IF;
END;
/

4.

DECLARE
   v_num1          NUMBER (8)    := &number1;
   v_num2          NUMBER (8)    := &number2;
   v_symbol        VARCHAR2 (1) := '&symbol';
   v_calculation   NUMBER (8);
BEGIN
   IF v_symbol = '+'
   THEN
      v_calculation   := v_num1 + v_num2;
   ELSIF v_symbol = '-'
   THEN


      v_calculation   := v_num1 - v_num2;
   ELSIF v_symbol = '*'
   THEN
      v_calculation   := v_num1 * v_num2;
   ELSIF v_symbol = '/'
   THEN
      v_calculation   := v_num1 / v_num2;
   END IF;

   DBMS_OUTPUT.put_line (v_calculation);
END;
/
```

5.

ELSEIF should be replaced by ELSIF.

Chapter 6 Iterative loop structures

1.

```
--SIMPLE LOOP
DECLARE
   v_num    NUMBER;
BEGIN
   LOOP
      DBMS_OUTPUT.put_line ('LOOP EXAMPLE');
      v_num      := v_num + 1;
      EXIT WHEN v_num = 100;
   END LOOP;
END;
/

--FOR LOOP
BEGIN
   FOR i IN 1 .. 50
   LOOP
      DBMS_OUTPUT.put_line ('LOOP EXAMPLE');
   END LOOP;
END;
/


--WHILE LOOP
DECLARE
   v_num    NUMBER;
BEGIN
   WHILE v_num < 50
   LOOP
      DBMS_OUTPUT.put_line ('LOOP EXAMPLE');
      v_num      := v_num + 1;
   END LOOP;
END;
/
```

2.

```
--Program to pring sundays of year 2009
```

ANSWERS OF THE EXCERCISES

```
DECLARE
   v_date   DATE := '01-jan-2009';
BEGIN
   LOOP
      IF TO_CHAR (v_date, 'DY') = 'SUN'
      THEN
         DBMS_OUTPUT.put_line (TO_CHAR (v_date, 'DAY DDTH MONTH YYYY'));
      END IF;

      v_date   := v_date + 1;
      EXIT WHEN TO_CHAR (v_date, 'YYYY') = '2010';
   END LOOP;
END;
/
```

3.

```
--Program to print Sundays of year 2009 by using continue condition
--Note that this example will only run in oracle 11g
DECLARE
   v_date   DATE := '01-jan-2009';
BEGIN
   LOOP
      CONTINUE TO_CHAR (v_date, 'DY') != 'SUN';
         DBMS_OUTPUT.put_line (TO_CHAR (v_date, 'DAY DDTH MONTH YYYY'));
      v_date   := v_date + 1;
      EXIT WHEN TO_CHAR (v_date, 'YYYY') = '2010';
   END LOOP;
END;
/
```

4.

```
/*Program to print holidays of 2009, 20010 and 2011
  using nested loops*/
DECLARE
   v_year   DATE := '01-jAn-2009';
   v_date   DATE;
BEGIN
   FOR i IN 1 .. 3
   LOOP
      v_date   := v_year;

      LOOP
         IF TO_CHAR (v_date, 'DY') = 'SUN'
         THEN
            DBMS_OUTPUT.put_line (TO_CHAR (v_date, 'DAY DDTH MONTH YYYY'));
         END IF;

         v_date   := v_date + 1;
         EXIT WHEN TO_CHAR (v_date, 'YYYY') != TO_CHAR (v_year, 'YYYY');
      END LOOP;

      v_year   := ADD_MONTHS (v_year, 12);
   END LOOP;
```

INTRODUCTION TO PL/SQL   Page 250

ANSWERS OF THE EXCERCISES

```
END;
/
```

5.

```
BEGIN
    FOR i IN 1 .. 50
    LOOP
        DBMS_OUTPUT.put_line (i);
END;
/
```

Keyword END LOOP is missing.

Chapter 7 PL/SQL composite data types

1.

```
DECLARE
    dept_rec     dept%ROWTYPE;
BEGIN
    SELECT *
    INTO    dept_rec
    FROM    dept
    WHERE   deptno = 10;

    DBMS_OUTPUT.put_line (   dept_rec.deptno
                          || ' '
                          || dept_rec.dname
                          || ' '
                          || dept_rec.loc
                         );
END;
/
```

2.

```
DECLARE
    TYPE emp_dept_ty IS RECORD (
        empno     emp.empno%TYPE      NOT NULL := 10,
        ename     emp.ename%TYPE,
        deptno    dept.deptno%TYPE,
        dname     dept.dname%TYPE
    );

    emp_dept_tb    emp_dept_ty;
BEGIN
    SELECT empno,
           ename,
           e.deptno,
           dname
```

```
    INTO    emp_dept_tb.empno,
            emp_dept_tb.ename,
            emp_dept_tb.deptno,
            emp_dept_tb.dname
    FROM    emp e, dept d
    WHERE   e.deptno = d.deptno AND e.empno = 7900;

    DBMS_OUTPUT.put_line (    emp_dept_tb.empno
                          || CHR (10)
                          || emp_dept_tb.ename
                          || CHR (10)
                          || emp_dept_tb.deptno

                          || CHR (10)
                          || emp_dept_tb.dname
                         );
END;
/
```

Note: CHR(10) is a new line indicator(carriage return).

Chapter 8 PL/SQL collections

1.

```
DECLARE
    TYPE count_ty IS TABLE OF VARCHAR2 (40)
        INDEX BY BINARY_INTEGER;

    count_tab       count_ty;
    v_date          DATE
                    := TO_DATE ('01' || TO_CHAR (SYSDATE, 'mmrrrr'), 'ddmmrrrr');
    v_last_day      NUMBER  := TO_NUMBER (TO_CHAR (LAST_DAY (SYSDATE), 'DD'));
BEGIN
    --Loop assigns 10 values at the same position as the index number
    FOR i IN 1 .. v_last_day
    LOOP
        count_tab (i)    := TO_CHAR (v_date, 'day ddth month');
        v_date           := v_date + 1;
    END LOOP;

-- loop to get the values of table count_tab
    FOR i IN 1 .. v_last_day
    LOOP
        DBMS_OUTPUT.put_line (count_tab (i));
    END LOOP;
END;
/
```

ANSWERS OF THE EXCERCISES

2.

Two dimension array
```
DECLARE
    TYPE month_col_ty IS RECORD (
        v_dd     NUMBER,
        v_day    VARCHAR2 (20)
    );

    TYPE count_ty IS TABLE OF month_col_ty
        INDEX BY BINARY_INTEGER;

    count_tab       count_ty;
    v_date          DATE
                    := TO_DATE ('01' || TO_CHAR (SYSDATE, 'mmrrrr'), 'ddmmrrrr');
    v_last_day      NUMBER   := TO_NUMBER (TO_CHAR (LAST_DAY (SYSDATE), 'DD'));
BEGIN
    --Loop assigns 10 values at the same position as the index number
    FOR i IN 1 .. v_last_day
    LOOP
        count_tab (i).v_dd      := i;
        count_tab (i).v_day     := TO_CHAR (v_date, 'DAY');
        v_date                  := v_date + 1;
    END LOOP;

-- loop to get the values of table count_tab
    FOR i IN 1 .. v_last_day
    LOOP
        DBMS_OUTPUT.put_line (count_tab (i).v_dd || ' ' || count_tab (i).v_day);
    END LOOP;
END;
/
```
Nested table

```
DECLARE
    TYPE month_col_ty IS RECORD (
        v_dd     NUMBER,
        v_day    VARCHAR2 (20)
    );

    TYPE count_ty IS TABLE OF month_col_ty;

    count_tab       count_ty := count_ty ();
    v_date          DATE
                    := TO_DATE ('01' || TO_CHAR (SYSDATE, 'mmrrrr'), 'ddmmrrrr');
    v_last_day      NUMBER   := TO_NUMBER (TO_CHAR (LAST_DAY (SYSDATE), 'DD'));
BEGIN
    --Loop assigns 10 values at the same position as the index number
    FOR i IN 1 .. v_last_day

    LOOP
        count_tab.EXTEND;
        count_tab (i).v_dd      := i;
        count_tab (i).v_day     := TO_CHAR (v_date, 'DAY');
        v_date                  := v_date + 1;
```

INTRODUCTION TO PL/SQL   Page 253

```
   END LOOP;

-- loop to get the values of table count_tab
   FOR i IN 1 .. v_last_day
   LOOP
      DBMS_OUTPUT.put_line (count_tab (i).v_dd || ' ' || count_tab (i).v_day);
   END LOOP;
END;
/
```

Varray

```
DECLARE
   TYPE month_col_ty IS RECORD (
      v_dd      NUMBER,
      v_day     VARCHAR2 (20)
   );

   TYPE count_ty IS VARRAY (31) OF month_col_ty;

   count_tab     count_ty := count_ty ();
   v_date        DATE
                    := TO_DATE ('01' || TO_CHAR (SYSDATE, 'mmrrrr'), 'ddmmrrrr');
   v_last_day    NUMBER   := TO_NUMBER (TO_CHAR (LAST_DAY (SYSDATE), 'DD'));
BEGIN
   --Loop assigns 10 values at the same position as the index number
   FOR i IN 1 .. v_last_day
   LOOP
      count_tab.EXTEND;
      count_tab (i).v_dd      := i;
      count_tab (i).v_day     := TO_CHAR (v_date, 'DAY');
      v_date                  := v_date + 1;
   END LOOP;

-- loop to get the values of table count_tab
   FOR i IN 1 .. v_last_day
   LOOP
      DBMS_OUTPUT.put_line (count_tab (i).v_dd || ' ' || count_tab (i).v_day);
   END LOOP;
END;
/
```

Chapter 9 Cursors

1.

Cursor is not opened by using OPEN statement.

2.

```
--Cursor usage to authenticate user
DECLARE
    --cursor with parameters
    CURSOR cur_security (p_name VARCHAR2, p_passw VARCHAR2)
    IS
        SELECT 1
        FROM   users
        WHERE  user_name = p_name AND PASSWORD = p_passw;

  -- cursor accepts username and passworld throung substitution variables
    v_username   VARCHAR2 (50)            := '&USERNAME';
    v_password   VARCHAR2 (25)            := '&PASSWORD';
    v_rec        cur_security%ROWTYPE;
BEGIN
    OPEN cur_security (v_username, v_password);

    LOOP
        FETCH cur_security
        INTO  v_rec;

        EXIT WHEN cur_security%NOTFOUND;
        DBMS_OUTPUT.put_line ('PROVIDE USER ACCESS');
    END LOOP;
    CLOSE cur_security;
END;
/
```

3.

```
--Example of cursor for loop
DECLARE
    CURSOR cur_security (p_name VARCHAR2, p_passw VARCHAR2)
    IS
        SELECT 1
        FROM   users
        WHERE  user_name = p_name AND PASSWORD = p_passw;

    v_username   VARCHAR2 (50)            := '&USERNAME';
    v_password   VARCHAR2 (25)            := '&PASSWORD';


    v_rec        cur_security%ROWTYPE;
BEGIN
    FOR v_rec IN cur_security (v_username, v_password)
    LOOP
        DBMS_OUTPUT.put_line ('PROVIDE USER ACCESS');
    END LOOP;
END;
/
```

ANSWERS OF THE EXCERCISES

4.

```
--Usage of where current of cursor
DECLARE
    CURSOR cur_dept
    IS
        SELECT      *
        FROM        dept
        WHERE       deptno = 10
        FOR UPDATE;
BEGIN
    FOR v_rec IN cur_dept
    LOOP
        UPDATE dept
        SET dname = 'FINANCE'
        WHERE CURRENT OF cur_dept;
    END LOOP;
END;
/
```

Chapter 10 Exception handling

1.

```
--Handling no_data_found exception
DECLARE
    v_name    VARCHAR2 (50);
BEGIN
    SELECT ename
    INTO   v_name
    FROM   emp e
    WHERE  e.empno = 5286;

    DBMS_OUTPUT.put_line (v_name);
EXCEPTION
    WHEN NO_DATA_FOUND
    THEN
        DBMS_OUTPUT.put_line ('No employee exists with this number');
END;
/
```

2.

```
DECLARE
    v_name    VARCHAR2 (50);
BEGIN
    SELECT ename
    INTO   v_name
    FROM   emp e;
    DBMS_OUTPUT.put_line (v_name);
END;

--Handling TO_MANY_ROWS exception
DECLARE
    v_name    VARCHAR2 (50);
BEGIN
    SELECT ename
    INTO   v_name
    FROM   emp e;

    DBMS_OUTPUT.put_line (v_name);
EXCEPTION
    WHEN too_many_rows
    THEN
        DBMS_OUTPUT.put_line ('Query is returning more then one row');
END;
/
```

3.

Just swap the order of DELETE queries, delete the child records first

```
DECLARE
    v_exp    EXCEPTION;
    PRAGMA EXCEPTION_INIT (v_exp, -2292);
BEGIN
    DELETE FROM emp
    WHERE       deptno = 20;

    DELETE FROM dept
    WHERE       deptno = 20;

    DBMS_OUTPUT.put_line ('Dept deleted');
EXCEPTION
    WHEN v_exp
    THEN
        DBMS_OUTPUT.put_line
                    ('Can not delete the record, while the child records exist');
END;
/
```

4.

```
--Example of user defined exception
DECLARE
    v_sal    emp.sal%TYPE;
    v_exp    EXCEPTION;
BEGIN
    SELECT sal
    INTO    v_sal
    FROM    emp
    WHERE   empno = '&empno';

    IF v_sal > 5000
    THEN
        RAISE v_exp;
    END IF;

    DBMS_OUTPUT.put_line (v_sal);
EXCEPTION
    WHEN v_exp
    THEN
        DBMS_OUTPUT.put_line ('Salary is greater then 5000 sal is ' || v_sal);
END;
/
```

5.

```
--user defined example by using raise_application_error
DECLARE
    v_sal    emp.sal%TYPE;
    v_exp    EXCEPTION;
BEGIN
    SELECT sal
    INTO   v_sal
    FROM   emp
    WHERE  empno = '&empno';

    IF v_sal > 5000
    THEN
        raise_application_error (-20040,
                                 'Salary is greater than 5000, sal is ' || v_sal
                                );
    END IF;

    DBMS_OUTPUT.put_line (v_sal);
END;
/
```

6.

The exception handler WHEN_OTHERS should be at last in exception section.

Chapter 12 Procedures

1.

```
--Procedure to get the maximum salary of the employee
CREATE OR REPLACE PROCEDURE max_sal (p_deptno NUMBER, p_sal OUT NUMBER)
IS
    v_max_sal    emp.sal%TYPE;
BEGIN
    SELECT MAX (sal)
    INTO   p_sal
    FROM   emp
    WHERE  deptno = p_deptno;
END;
/

SQL> VARIABLE G_SAL NUMBER
SQL> EXECUTE MAX_SAL(10,:G_SAL);


PL/SQL procedure successfully completed.
SQL> PRINT G_SAL
```

```
  G_SAL
----------
  5000
```

2.

```
--Procedure to get the maximum salary of the employee
--Using only one parameter
CREATE OR REPLACE PROCEDURE max_sal (p_dept_msal IN OUT NUMBER)
IS
   v_max_sal    emp.sal%TYPE;
BEGIN
   SELECT MAX (sal)
   INTO   p_dept_msal
   FROM   emp
   WHERE  deptno = p_dept_msal;
END;
/

SQL> VARIABLE G_SAL NUMBER
SQL> BEGIN :G_SAL:=10; END;
PL/SQL procedure successfully completed.
SQL> EXECUTE MAX_SAL(:G_SAL);
PL/SQL procedure successfully completed.
SQL> PRINT G_SAL

  G_SAL
----------
  5000

--Call the procedure from PL/SQL block
DECLARE
   v_sal    NUMBER (10) := 10;
BEGIN
   max_sal (v_sal);
   DBMS_OUTPUT.put_line (v_sal);
END;
/
```

3.

The exception is not handled in the procedure and propagates in the calling programe and ignores all the executable statement, To execute the calling programe successfully handel the exception in the procedure itself as following.

```
CREATE OR REPLACE PROCEDURE get_info (p_empno NUMBER)
IS
   v_sal     NUMBER (6);
   v_name    VARCHAR2 (30);
BEGIN
   SELECT ename,
```

```
        sal
   INTO    v_name,
           v_sal
   FROM    emp
   WHERE   empno = p_empno;

   DBMS_OUTPUT.put_line (v_name || ' ' || TO_NUMBER (v_sal));
EXCEPTION
   WHEN NO_DATA_FOUND
   THEN
      DBMS_OUTPUT.put_line ('Employee does not exists');

END;
/

BEGIN
   get_info (79);
   DBMS_OUTPUT.put_line ('CALLING PROCEDURE');
END;
```

4.

Parameter with IN mode can never be used as target of an assignment as value is being assigned to P_EMPNO in executable section.

Chapter 13 Functions

1.

```
CREATE OR REPLACE FUNCTION emp_sal (p_empno NUMBER)
   RETURN NUMBER
IS
   v_sal    NUMBER;
BEGIN
   SELECT sal
   INTO    v_sal
   FROM    emp
   WHERE   empno = p_empno;

   RETURN (v_sal);
END; /
```

Using ISQL*PLUS
VARIABLE g_sal NUMBER;
EXECUTE g_sal=emp_sal(7900);
PRINT g_sal
Using PL/SQL block

```
BEGIN
   DBMS_OUTPUT.put_line ('Salary is ' || TO_CHAR (emp_sal (7900)));
END;
```

2.

```
CREATE OR REPLACE FUNCTION my_convertor (p_value NUMBER, p_unit VARCHAR2)
   RETURN VARCHAR2
IS
BEGIN
   IF p_unit = 'M'
   THEN
      RETURN (   TO_CHAR (p_value)
              || 'KM= '
              || TO_CHAR (p_value * 1000)
              || ' meters'
             );
   ELSIF p_unit = 'F'
   THEN
      RETURN ((9 / 5) * p_value + 32);
   ELSE
      RETURN NULL;
   END IF;
END;
/
```

```
BEGIN
   DBMS_OUTPUT.put_line (my_convert (2, 'M'));
END;
```

3.

```
--Function the will return the number of days,weeks or years
--since the Date of birth of a user
CREATE OR REPLACE FUNCTION cal_age_days (dob DATE, p_flag VARCHAR2)
   RETURN NUMBER
IS
   v_days    NUMBER;
BEGIN
   SELECT SYSDATE - dob
   INTO   v_days
   FROM   DUAL;

   IF p_flag = 'D'
   THEN
      RETURN round(v_days);
   ELSIF p_flag = 'W'
   THEN
      RETURN round(v_days / 7);
   ELSIF p_flag = 'Y'
   THEN
      RETURN round(v_days / 365);
   ELSE
      RETURN 0;
```

```
   END IF;
END;
/

--Test
SELECT cal_age_days (TO_DATE ('31-01-1983', 'dd-mm-rrrr'), 'Y')
FROM   DUAL
/
```

4.

A function cannot be called inside a SQL expression when it contains a DML statement. Read "Restrictions on calling functions from SQL expressions".

Chapter 14 Subprogram management

1.

'FARHAN' will not be able to execute the procedure because the procedure executes under the security privileges of the caller when the setting is AUTHID CURRENT_USER, either replace it with AUTHID DEFINER or assign SELECT privilege of EMP table to 'FARHAN'.

2.

There is no difference because AUTHID DEFINER is default setting so if AUTHID DEFINER is not given still procedure will be created with this.

3.

```
SELECT text
FROM   user_source
WHERE  NAME = 'EMP_PROCEDURE';
/
```

4.

```
SELECT object_name,
       object_type
FROM   user_objects
```

Chapter 15 Packages

1.

```
--Package specification
CREATE OR REPLACE PACKAGE comm_pkg
IS
--Procedure will give 10% commission
-- to the employee who has sal less then 8000
    PROCEDURE emp_com (p_empno NUMBER);
END;
/

----------------------
----------------------
--package body

CREATE OR REPLACE PACKAGE BODY comm_pkg
IS
    --Privat function
--Function will return True, if the employee's
--salary is less then 8000
    FUNCTION emp_com_elgible (p_empno NUMBER)
        RETURN BOOLEAN
    IS
        v_sal   NUMBER (10);
    BEGIN
        SELECT sal
        INTO   v_sal
        FROM   emp
        WHERE  empno = p_empno;

        IF v_sal > 8000
        THEN
            RETURN FALSE;
        ELSE
            RETURN TRUE;
        END IF;
    EXCEPTION
        WHEN NO_DATA_FOUND
        THEN
            RETURN FALSE;
    END;

----------------
    PROCEDURE emp_com (p_empno NUMBER)
    IS
    BEGIN
        --If the employee is elgible give him commission


        IF emp_com_elgible (p_empno)
        THEN
            UPDATE emp
            SET comm = sal * .10
```

```
            WHERE   empno = p_empno;

            COMMIT;
        ELSE
            raise_application_error (-20050, 'Not elgible of commission');
        END IF;
    END;
END;
/
```

2.

```
--Overloading Example
 create or replace package overload_pkg
 is
procedure raise_sal(p_emp number);
procedure raise_sal(p_emp number,p_percent number);
 end;
 /
-------------------------------------------------
--Overloading Example
create or replace package body overload_pkg
is
procedure raise_sal(p_emp number)
is
begin
update emp
set sal=sal+(sal*.10)
where empno=p_emp;
end;
procedure raise_sal(p_emp number,p_percent number)
is
begin
update emp
set sal=sal+(sal*(p_percent/100))
where empno=p_emp;
end;
end;
/
```

3.

Function should be written before procedure or forward referencing should be used.

4.

```
--Use forward referencing as following
CREATE OR REPLACE PACKAGE BODY comm_pkg
IS
--Use forwarding Refering
    FUNCTION emp_com_elgible (p_empno NUMBER)
        RETURN BOOLEAN;
    PROCEDURE emp_com (p_empno NUMBER)
    IS
```

ANSWERS OF THE EXCERCISES

```
    BEGIN
        --If the employee is elgible give him commission
        IF emp_com_elgible (p_empno)
        THEN
            UPDATE emp
            SET comm = sal * .10
            WHERE  empno = p_empno;

            COMMIT;
        ELSE
            raise_application_error (-20050, 'Not elgible of commission');
        END IF;
    END;
-----------------------
    --Privat function
--Function will return True, if the employee's
--salary is less then 8000
    FUNCTION emp_com_elgible (p_empno NUMBER)
        RETURN BOOLEAN
    IS
        v_sal    NUMBER (10);
    BEGIN
        SELECT sal
        INTO   v_sal
        FROM   emp
        WHERE  empno = p_empno;

        IF v_sal > 8000
        THEN
            RETURN FALSE;
        ELSE
            RETURN TRUE;
        END IF;
    EXCEPTION
        WHEN NO_DATA_FOUND


        THEN
            RETURN FALSE;
    END;
END;
/


5.


--Onetime only procedure
Create or replace package onetm_only_pkg
is
v_sal number(10);
procedure print_sal;
end;
/

create or replace package body onetm_only_pkg
is
procedure print_sal
is
```

```
begin
dbms_output.put_line(v_sal);
end;
begin
select sal
into v_sal
from emp
where empno=7900;
end;
/
```

6.

Replace the END keyword of the onetime only procedure

7.

Because the procedure is overloaded and parameters names are also same so the data types of the parameter can not belong to same family, NUMBER and INTEGER belong to same family.

Chapter 16Triggers

1.

```
--Trigger to keep the history of deleted records into emp_his table
--Delete one record from emp table and see that record into emp_his table
CREATE OR REPLACE TRIGGER emp_update_info
    BEFORE DELETE
    ON emp
    FOR EACH ROW
BEGIN
    --contains date of updation and the user name who updated
    INSERT INTO emp_his
                (empno,
                 ename,
                 job,
                 mgr,
                 hiredate,
                 sal,
                 comm,
                 deptno
                )
    VALUES      (:OLD.empno,
                 :OLD.ename,
                 :OLD.job,
                 :OLD.mgr,
                 :OLD.hiredate,
                 :OLD.sal,
                 :OLD.comm,
```

```
                    :OLD.deptno
               );
END;
/
```

2.

```
-- Trigger to insert the DML information into new table
CREATE OR REPLACE TRIGGER emp_dml_his
    BEFORE UPDATE OR INSERT OR DELETE
    ON emp
BEGIN
    INSERT INTO emp_dml_info
               (c_date,
                c_user
               )
    VALUES     (SYSDATE,
                USER
               );END;/
```

3.

```
--Performing the action according to the DML operation
CREATE OR REPLACE TRIGGER emp_dml_his
    BEFORE UPDATE OR INSERT OR DELETE
    ON emp
BEGIN
    IF UPDATING
    THEN
        INSERT INTO emp_dml_info
                   (c_date,
                    c_user
                   )
        VALUES     (SYSDATE,
                    USER || ', UPDATION HAS BEEN PERFORMED'
                   );
    ELSIF INSERTING
    THEN
        INSERT INTO emp_dml_info
                   (c_date,
                    c_user
                   )
        VALUES     (SYSDATE,
                    USER || ', INSERTION HAS BEEN PERFORMED'
                   );
    ELSIF DELETING
    THEN
        INSERT INTO emp_dml_info
                   (c_date,
                    c_user
                   )
        VALUES     (SYSDATE,
                    USER || ', DELETION HAS BEEN PERFORMED'
```

```
                            );
    END IF;
END;
/
```

4.

Since it is a compound trigger so clause 'COMPOUND TRIGGER' is missing, the statement should be like following

```
CREATE OR REPLACE TRIGGER COMP_TRIGG
FOR UPDATE ON EMP
COMPOUND TRIGGER
AFTER STATEMENT IS
BEGIN
INSERT INTO emp_upd_info
                (date_upd,
                 user_upd
                 )
    VALUES      (SYSDATE,
                 USER
                 );
END;
END
/
```

5.

As the view is simple view so no need to create an instead of trigger, DML operation can be performed normally.

Chapter 17 Using Oracle Object types

1.

```
CREATE TYPE obj_type IS OBJECT (
    empno     NUMBER (10),
    ename     VARCHAR2 (30),
    gender    VARCHAR2 (8)
);

CREATE  TABLE obj_table(deptno NUMBER(10),emp obj_type)
/
INSERT INTO obj_table
VALUES      (1,
                 obj_type (1, 'FARHAN', 'MALE')
                 )
/
INSERT INTO obj_table
VALUES      (1,
```

```
                obj_type (2, 'ALIZA', 'FEMALE')
                )
/
INSERT INTO obj_table
VALUES      (1,
                obj_type (3, 'IMRAN', 'MALE')
                )
/
SELECT deptno,
       t.emp.empno,
       t.emp.ename,
       t.emp.gender
FROM   obj_table t
/
UPDATE obj_table t
SET t.emp.ename = 'FARHAN ALI'
WHERE  t.emp.ename = 'FARHAN'
/
```

2.

```
--Use of object type to declare record variable
DECLARE
   v_obj_type   obj_type := obj_type (1, 'HIRA', 'FEMALE');
BEGIN
   SELECT t.emp.empno,
          t.emp.ename,
          t.emp.gender
   INTO   v_obj_type.empno,
          v_obj_type.ename,
          v_obj_type.gender
   FROM   obj_table t
   WHERE  t.emp.ename = 'FARHAN ALI';

   DBMS_OUTPUT.put_line (   v_obj_type.empno
                         || ' '
                         || v_obj_type.ename
                         || ' '
                         || v_obj_type.gender
                        );
END;
/
```

3.

```
--Member method example
CREATE OR REPLACE TYPE obj_type2 AS OBJECT (
    deptno    NUMBER (6),
    emp       obj_type,
    MEMBER PROCEDURE display_address (SELF IN OUT obj_type2)
)
/

--Body of the object type to implement method
CREATE OR REPLACE TYPE BODY obj_type2
AS
    MEMBER PROCEDURE display_address (SELF IN OUT NOCOPY obj_type2)
    IS
    BEGIN
        DBMS_OUTPUT.put_line (deptno || ' ' || emp.empno || ' ' || emp.ename);
    END;
END;
/

--Usage of the member method
DECLARE
    v_dis_add    obj_type2;
BEGIN
    v_dis_add    := obj_type2 (1, obj_type (1, 'FARHAN', 'MALE'));
    v_dis_add.display_address ();
END;
/
```

4.

```
CREATE OR REPLACE TYPE obj_type3 AS OBJECT (
    v_var    NUMBER,
    STATIC PROCEDURE ID (p_number NUMBER)
);
/

CREATE OR REPLACE TYPE BODY obj_type3
AS
    STATIC PROCEDURE ID (p_number NUMBER)
    IS
    BEGIN
        DBMS_OUTPUT.put_line ('This is a static method');
        DBMS_OUTPUT.put_line (p_number);
    END;
END;
/


EXEC obj_type3.id(14);
```

ANSWERS OF THE EXCERCISES

5.

```
--Object created that resembles to emp table
--Note the %ROWTYPE cannot be used with nested tables declared
--at database level so each column is declared individually.

CREATE OR REPLACE TYPE emp_rec_type AS OBJECT (
    empno       NUMBER (4),
    ename       VARCHAR2 (30),
    job         VARCHAR2 (27),
    mgr         NUMBER (4),
    hiredate    DATE,
    sal         NUMBER (12, 3),
    comm        NUMBER (7, 2),
    deptno      NUMBER (2),
    age         NUMBER
)
/

--Nested table creation based on object type

CREATE OR REPLACE TYPE emp_tab_type AS TABLE OF emp_rec_type;
/

--Table cration that hold dept table columns and collumns of emp table
CREATE TABLE dept_emp_table(deptno NUMBER(2) NOT NULL,
dname                                    VARCHAR2(42),
loc                                      VARCHAR2(39),
emp                                      emp_tab_type)
NESTED TABLE emp STORE AS emp_tab_nt
/
--New record inserted that has multiple employees against one department
INSERT INTO dept_emp_table
VALUES        (1,
              'IT',
              'DUBAI',
              emp_tab_type (emp_rec_type (1,
                                          'FARHAN',
                                          'APPLICATION DEVELOPER',
                                          2,
                                          '01-FEB-2009',
                                          8000,
                                          NULL,
                                          1,
                                          25
                                          ),
                            emp_rec_type (2,


                                          'ALI',
                                          'APPLICATION DEVELOPER',
                                          2,
                                          '01-FEB-2008',
                                          9000,
                                          NULL,
                                          1,
```

```
                                        25
                                      )
                          )
              )
/
--Record Access through PL/SQL

DECLARE
    v_emp_tab       emp_tab_type;
    v_deptno        emp.deptno%TYPE;
    v_dname         dept.dname%TYPE;
    v_loc           dept.loc%TYPE;
BEGIN
    SELECT deptno,
           dname,
           loc,
           emp
    INTO   v_deptno,
           v_dname,
           v_loc,
           v_emp_tab
    FROM   dept_emp_table;

    FOR i IN v_emp_tab.FIRST .. v_emp_tab.LAST
    LOOP
        DBMS_OUTPUT.put_line (      'DEPTNO='
                                ||  v_deptno
                                ||  ' DEPTNAME='
                                ||  v_dname
                                ||  ' LOC='
                                ||  v_loc
                                ||  ' EMPNO='
                                ||  v_emp_tab (i).empno
                                ||  ' ENAME='
                                ||  v_emp_tab (i).ename
                                ||  ' SAL='
                                ||  v_emp_tab (i).sal
                             );
    END LOOP;
END;
/

--Select all columns of all records


SELECT *
FROM   dept_emp_table
/
--Record acess through SQL
SELECT empno,
       ename,
       sal
FROM   TABLE (SELECT emp
                FROM   dept_emp_table)
/
```

6.

```
--Updating record in nested table
UPDATE TABLE (SELECT emp
             FROM   dept_emp_table t
             WHERE  deptno = 1)
SET ename = 'ALI NOOR'
WHERE   empno = 2
/
--To delete a complete row of emp
DELETE FROM TABLE (SELECT emp
                  FROM   dept_emp_table t
                  WHERE  deptno = 1)
WHERE        empno = 2
/

--Inserting a new record
INSERT INTO TABLE (SELECT emp
                  FROM   dept_emp_table t
                  WHERE  deptno = 1)
VALUES       (emp_rec_type (2,
                           'ALI',
                           'APPLICATION DEVELOPER',
                           2,
                           '01-FEB-2008',
                           9000,
                           NULL,
                           1,
                           25
                           )
             )
/
```

7.

The VARRAY can have only 10 elements while the statement is trying to assign 15 elements, either increase the VARRAYs size or assign 10 values maximum.

Chapter 18 Bulk SQL

1.

```
--Example of bulk SQL
--Create a table emp_test as following
--Create tabel emp_test as select * from emp where 1=2
DECLARE
    TYPE v_emp_ty IS TABLE OF emp%ROWTYPE
        INDEX BY PLS_INTEGER;

    v_emp    v_emp_ty;
    v_st     NUMBER;
    v_et     NUMBER;
BEGIN
    v_st     := DBMS_UTILITY.get_time ();

    SELECT *
    BULK COLLECT INTO v_emp
    FROM    emp;

    FORALL i IN v_emp.FIRST .. v_emp.LAST
        INSERT INTO emp_test
        VALUES        v_emp (i);
    v_et     := DBMS_UTILITY.get_time ();
    DBMS_OUTPUT.put_line ('Total time ' || TO_CHAR (v_et - v_st));
END;
/

Output
Total time 0
PL/SQL Procedure successfully completed

--Insets data in table emp_test without bulk collect
DECLARE
    CURSOR c_cur
    IS
        SELECT *
        FROM    emp;

    TYPE employees_t IS TABLE OF emp%ROWTYPE

        INDEX BY PLS_INTEGER;

    retirees    employees_t;
    v_st        NUMBER;
    v_et        NUMBER;
BEGIN
    v_st     := DBMS_UTILITY.get_time ();

    FOR rec IN c_cur
    LOOP
        retirees (NVL (c_cur%ROWCOUNT, 1))        := rec;
        DBMS_OUTPUT.put_line (TO_NUMBER (c_cur%ROWCOUNT) || '1');
```

```
    END LOOP;

    FOR indx IN retirees.FIRST .. retirees.LAST
    LOOP
        INSERT INTO emp_test
        VALUES        retirees (indx);
    END LOOP;

    v_et     := DBMS_UTILITY.get_time ();
    DBMS_OUTPUT.put_line ('Total time ' || TO_CHAR (v_et - v_st));
END;
/

Output
Total time 1
PL/SQL Procedure successfully completed
```

Note: You will get large difference with huge data, as here I have executed it against 10 rows only

2.

1 Create a new table emp_test2 as
CRATE TABLE emp_test2 AS SELECT * FROM emp where 1=2;

2 Modify table emp_test's column empno to varchar2
ALTER TABLE emp_test modify(empno VARCHAR2(5));

3 insert emp table's data in emp_test
INSERT INTO emp_test(SELECT * from emp);

3 create PLSQL block
```
--Block for handling BULK EXCEPTIONS
DECLARE
    CURSOR c_cur IS SELECT  *  FROM    emp_test;


    bulk_errors    EXCEPTION;
    PRAGMA EXCEPTION_INIT (bulk_errors, -24381);
    TYPE employees_t IS TABLE OF emp%ROWTYPE
        INDEX BY PLS_INTEGER;
v_emp       employees_t;
BEGIN
    FOR rec IN c_cur
    LOOP
        v_emp (NVL (c_cur%ROWCOUNT, 1))        := rec;
        END LOOP;
FORALL indx IN v_emp.FIRST .. v_emp.LAST SAVE EXCEPTIONS
        INSERT INTO emp_test2
        VALUES        retirees (indx);
EXCEPTION
    WHEN bulk_errors
```

```
        THEN
            FOR j IN 1 .. SQL%BULK_EXCEPTIONS.COUNT
            LOOP
                DBMS_OUTPUT.put_line
                                    (    'Error from element #'
                                    ||   TO_CHAR (SQL%BULK_EXCEPTIONS (j).ERROR_INDEX)
                                    ||   ': '
                                    ||   SQLERRM (SQL%BULK_EXCEPTIONS (j).ERROR_CODE)
                                    );
            END LOOP;
END;
/

Output
Error from element #2:   -1722: non-ORACLE exception
PL/SQL procedure successfully completed.
```

3.

```
DECLARE
    TYPE v_num_type IS TABLE OF NUMBER
        INDEX BY BINARY_INTEGER;
    v_num    v_num_type;
BEGIN
    UPDATE      TEST
    SET v_counter = 1
    WHERE       v_counter = 2
    RETURNING v_counter
    INTO BULK COLLECT v_num;   --this clause was missing
    DBMS_OUTPUT.put_line ('Rows deleted: ' || SQL%ROWCOUNT);
    FOR i IN v_num.FIRST .. v_num.LAST
    LOOP
        DBMS_OUTPUT.put_line ('Row ' || v_num (i));
    END LOOP;
END;/
```

Chapter 19 Dynamic SQL

1.

```
--Dynamic SQL
DECLARE
    v_dept    VARCHAR2 (50) := 'DELETe FROM DEPT WHERE DEPTno=10';
BEGIN
    EXECUTE IMMEDIATE v_dept;

    DBMS_OUTPUT.put_line (SQL%ROWCOUNT || ' Rows deleted');
END;
```

ANSWERS OF THE EXCERCISES

2.

The bind variable is missing in the string, it should be as following.

```
DECLARE
   v_string   VARCHAR2 (200) := 'select ename into :ename from emp where empno=:empno';
   v_name     VARCHAR2 (30);
   p_empno    NUMBER        :=7900;
BEGIN
   EXECUTE IMMEDIATE v_string
   INTO        v_name
   USING       p_empno;
   DBMS_OUTPUT.put_line ('Employee is ' || v_name);
END;
/
```

3.

```
--Dynamic SQL
DECLARE
   TYPE empctyp IS REF CURSOR;

   emp_c      empctyp;
   v_ename    VARCHAR2 (15);
   v_sal      NUMBER;
   v_comm     NUMBER;
   p_sal      NUMBER          := 1000;
BEGIN
   OPEN emp_c FOR                                        -- open cursor variable
               'SELECT ename, sal, COMM FROM emp WHERE sal > :s' USING
   p_sal;

LOOP
      FETCH emp_c
      INTO  v_ename,
            v_sal,
            v_comm;

      EXIT WHEN emp_c%NOTFOUND;
      DBMS_OUTPUT.put_line (    'Name '
                            || v_ename
                            || ' Salary '
                            || v_sal
                            || ' Comm '
                            || v_comm
                           );
      v_sal    := v_sal + 1000; --Added 1000 in salary
      DBMS_OUTPUT.put_line ('Name ' || v_ename || ' Salary ' || v_sal);
   END LOOP;
```

```
    CLOSE emp_c;
END;
/
```

4.

```
--Usage of refcursor
-- IS REF CURSOR was written as IS CURSOR in declaration section
DECLARE
    TYPE emp_ref_c_ty IS REF CURSOR;

    emp_ref_c      emp_ref_c_ty;
    v_empno        emp.empno%TYPE;
    v_ename        emp.ename%TYPE;
    v_string       VARCHAR2 (200)    := '&P_String';
BEGIN
    OPEN emp_ref_c FOR v_string;

    LOOP
        FETCH emp_ref_c
        INTO  v_empno,
              v_ename;

        EXIT WHEN emp_ref_c%NOTFOUND;
        DBMS_OUTPUT.put_line (v_empno || '  ' || v_ename);
    END LOOP;

    CLOSE emp_ref_c;
END;
/
```

This Page is intentionally left blank

INDEX

A

Associative Array, 58
Associative Array Two dimensional, 62
Attributes, 75
Automatic, 212

B

Bind, 108
Body, 134
Bodiless, 139

C

Characteristic, 7
Close, 75
Collections, 58, 67, 69, 171
Comments, 11
Compound, 39, 167
Compound Symbols, 9
Composite, 54, 58, 114
Conditional, 32
Continue, 50
Conversion, 22
Counter, 45
Cross Session, 212
Cursors, 73
Cursor FOR LOOP 83, 84
Cursor Variable, 89

D

Data dictionary, 127
Data Type, 15
Declaring, 3, 174
Definer's right, 129

Delimiters, 8
DML, 29
Drop, 116,123, 140
Dynamic SQL, 196, 200, 210

E

Enhancements, 68, 211
Explicit Cursors, 73, 74
Exception, 93
Exception Section, 2
Executable Section, 2
Extend, 65

F

Function, 119
Fetching, 74, 195
FORALL, 188
FOR LOOP, 45, 83
Forward Declaration, 144

H

Handle, 112
Host, 105

I

Identifiers, 10
Implicit Conversion, 22
IF-THEN, 32
IF-THEN-ELSIF, 35
Implicit Cursors, 73
INSTEAD OF trigger, 164
Invoking Subprograms, 104, 111
Iterative Loop, 42
INTO, 202

INDEX

INDEX